DISCIPLE

FAST TRACK

Becoming Disciples Through Bible Study

OLD TESTAMENT
STUDY MANUAL

DISCIPLE FAST TRACK
Old Testament Study Manual
Copyright © 2016 by Abingdon Press
DISCIPLE: BECOMING DISCIPLES THROUGH BIBLE STUDY
Study Manual, copyright © 1987 by Graded Press
Second Edition, copyright © 1993 by Abingdon Press
All rights reserved.

Writers: Richard Byrd Wilke and Julia Kitchens Wilke
Old Testament Consultant to the Writers: William J. A. Power
General Editor: Susan Wilke Fuquay
Design Manager and Illustrator: Keely Moore

20 21 22 23 24 25—10 9
Manufactured in the United States of America

DISCIPLE FAST TRACK

CONTENTS

As You Begin DISCIPLE FAST TRACK

You are committing yourself to at least three to four hours a week of independent study and preparation, plus seventy-five minutes each week in the weekly group meeting, for twenty-four weeks when you complete both the Old Testament and New Testament studies.

To establish a disciplined pattern of study, choose and stick to a particular time and location for daily reading and writing, study, reflection, and prayer.

Choosing a Bible

This Study Manual is based on the Common English Bible. We recommend *The CEB Study Bible: with Apocrypha*, edited by Joel B. Green (Common English Bible, 2013). Other excellent study Bibles and translations are available. Keep one or two handy for comparing difficult verses or passages.

Study Manual Format

This Study Manual is a discipline. It is a plan to guide your private study and preparation for the weekly group meeting.

Common elements appear throughout the lessons. The theme word, Scripture verse(s), and title at the beginning of each lesson suggest the subject and direction of the lesson. Together, they can help you remember the sequence of the biblical story.

"Our Human Condition" expresses a common human experience and provides a perspective from which to read and listen to Scripture.

Daily Bible reading assignments are listed and space is provided for making notes about the Scripture—key ideas, persons, events, new insights, geographic or historic information, the meaning of particular words, and questions you have about the Scripture that you want to raise in the group meeting.

Daily assignments also indicate when to read and respond to "The Bible Teaching" and the "Marks of Discipleship" sections of the lesson. The day on which you do this work will vary depending on the content of the lesson. The "Marks of Discipleship" identify particular characteristics of disciples and invite you to think about ways your life and the life of your congregation reflect those characteristics. Don't rush through this part of your work. It will be a valuable source of insight and discussion for you and members of the group.

"If You Want to Know More" suggests additional individual reading and study and the occasional preparation of a report to the group. The additional study resources suggested below will be helpful here.

As you begin your daily study, use the prayer psalm from the "Prayer" section. Write down concerns about which you will pray during the week.

Additional Study Resources

Though you need only the Bible and this Study Manual for successful study of DISCIPLE FAST TRACK, these reference books will help you go deeper into study of the Scriptures:

- *The CEB Bible: Bible Dictionary* (Common English Bible, Nashville, 2011)
- *The CEB Concise Concordance* (Common English Bible, 2012)
- *CEB Bible Map Guide* (Common English Bible, 2011)

How to Get the Most From Reading Scripture

- Read with curiosity. Ask the questions *who, what, where, when, how,* and *why* as you read.
- Learn as much as you can about the passage you are studying. It will help you hear God speak to you through the Scripture. Try to discover what the writer was saying for the time in which the passage was written. Read the surrounding verses and chapters to establish the setting or situation in which the action or teaching took place.
- Pay attention to the form of the passage, because meaning exists not only in what is said but in the form in which it is said. How you read and understand poetry or a parable will differ from how you read and understand historical narrative.
- Don't force your interpretation on the biblical text. Let the Scripture speak for itself.
- Question the Scripture, but also learn to read Scripture so you find answers to your questions in the Scripture itself. The biblical text will solve some of the problems you have with a particular passage. Some problems additional reference material will solve, and some will remain a mystery.
- Come to the Bible with an eagerness to listen to Scripture as the Word of God and a willingness to hear and obey it. Trust the Holy Spirit to instruct you and to empower you through Scripture.

DISCIPLE
FAST TRACK

OLD TESTAMENT

"God created humanity in God's own image, in the divine image God created them, male and female God created them."
—Genesis 1:27

1 The Creating God

OUR HUMAN CONDITION

I wonder who made me and my world. If there is a creator, what is this creator like? Why was I made? Scientists say some rocks are billions of years old and stars millions of light years away. In a universe so big, surely I am only a speck of dust. Does God really have anything to do with me? Does the Bible have any answers or power to offer me?

ASSIGNMENT

The goal of DISCIPLE FAST TRACK is to develop disciples of Jesus Christ who know and love God's Word. Throughout the study, you will be reading Scripture. As you read it, take notes and write down your reflections and/or questions in this study manual. Daily assignments will guide you in reading the Bible, the manual, and preparing you for your group.

PRAYER

Pray daily before study:

"Your hands have made me and set me in place.
Help me understand so I can learn your commandments" (Psalm 119:73).

Prayer concerns for the week:

Day 1 **One Bible:** many books with different styles of literature. Hold the Bible in your hands, remembering that it is many books by many writers who were inspired by God. Study the listing of the books of the Bible to get a feel for the titles. Locate study aids in your Bible, such as introductions, footnotes, maps, charts, and supplementary articles. Write your impressions.

Day 2 **Read Psalm 84** (poetry); **1 Chronicles 22** (history); **Exodus 20** (law). Consider which type of literature you enjoy most.

Day 3 **Read Micah 4** (prophets); **Philemon** (a letter from Paul); **Luke 15** (parables of Jesus). Consider which type of literature you enjoy most.

Day 4 **Read aloud Genesis 1:1–2:3** (the first Creation story), **then Genesis 2:4-25** (the second Creation story); **Psalm 8** (praise to the Creator).

Day 5 **Psalm 19:1-6** (God's glory); **Psalm 150** (praise); **Job 38** (God's mystery and majesty).

Day 6 **Read "The Bible Teaching" and the "Marks of Discipleship" and answer the questions.**

Day 7 **Rest, pray, and attend class.**

THE BIBLE TEACHING

The word *Bible* means "book." It is *the* book. All others pale beside it. Yet it is not a single book but a library of sixty-six books, written over a period of a thousand years. But the experiences that are recalled, analyzed, evaluated, and celebrated occurred over a much longer period. Stories were told around campfires; songs and psalms were sung in countless worship settings; histories were written and rewritten; laws received by inspiration were systematized and interpreted; prophecies were proclaimed, written down, fulfilled. Visions of a kingdom of justice and peace kept circulating through the people's minds.

The Bible tells about the Hebrew people. They were a unique people, unique in that they were called to be a revealing people, struggling always to be God's people, beginning about 2000 B.C. when Abram and Sarai heard the Lord call them to "go forth." God spoke in and through the experiences of this called people. Later, through the life, death, and resurrection of Jesus, God made full revelation and continued to show mysteries of truth with a new people of faith we call the church.

The Bible, inspired by God, is both human and divine. You may be surprised at how human the Bible is when you read of violence, rape, betrayal, adultery, sickness, and death. Nothing is hidden. You also will be overwhelmed at how divine the Bible is when you see repentance and faith, just and compassionate laws, acts of devotion and self-sacrifice, and the unending love of the forgiving, covenant God.

Not only are the experiences both human and divine, but so are the actual writings. Oral tradition was finally put into writing, then edited and reedited, copied and recopied; the whole process is a witness to the guiding hand of God. Even the canonizing—setting the standards for what is Scripture—was inspired.

When we speak of Scripture as being inspired, we are recognizing that the Scriptures were written by particular persons in particular circumstances. We are saying that the Scriptures are connected to God and, because of that connection, the Scriptures have power to bring about an encounter between God and the one who reads Scripture. The authority of Scripture, then, lies in its ability to cause encounter. When we read the Bible and God speaks to us, we hear the Bible as God's Word.

How Do We Read the Bible?

Our goal is not to learn the Bible as we learn algebra. Nor do we read a book of Scripture as we would read a detective story or a novel. Rather, as we read, we listen for the Holy Spirit to help us understand eternal, universal truths. We watch for unexpected insights that are personal, just for us. We savor a promise, thrill to a story that rings true in our experience, or agonize over a law or principle that could change our lives.

As our spiritual understanding grows, we see new truth. Also, as we live through experiences of sickness, sin, trial, and tragedy, we come to comprehend teachings we could never fathom before. But most important of all, the Holy Spirit will lead and guide you as you study. Jesus said, "The Companion, the Holy Spirit . . . will teach you everything and will remind you of everything I told you" (John 14:26).

Why Study the Bible?

What do you bring to the Bible? Your humanity. Everything you have ever thought, done, experienced, or agonized over can be dealt with by the Bible. Every human emotion is expressed there.

What do the Scriptures bring to you? God's authoritative guidance and counsel. The Bible has to express humanity in order to reach us; it has to express divinity in order to save us.

Once you gain familiarity with the Bible and are touched by God's Spirit, you will hunger and thirst for more of God's Word. What starts out as hard work turns into satisfaction and joy.

In the Beginning—The Bible Begins With Creation

The Hebrew verb for *create* refers to the activity of God, not to human activity (Genesis 1:1). Two ideas are contained in the verb *create*. First, God freely, purposefully creates order out of chaos. Second, God arranges and designs that creation.

"The heavens and the earth" means the immeasurable universe, all that was or is or ever will be.

"The earth was without shape or form, it was dark over the deep sea" (1:2) refers to a cosmic emptiness, a formless darkness, sometimes referred to as a "sea of chaos." The ancients believed that all creation originated from a dark, watery chaos, "the deep." Look up Psalm 24:1-2. "God's wind swept over the waters" (Genesis 1:2). Other translations for "swept" could be "hovered," "soared," or "trembled."

The Hebrews did not believe that the Creator was simply one of a group of gods. They did not believe that two gods, one good and one evil, battled to bring creation into existence. Rather, they believed that the one and only Lord of the universe, the one who had created them to be a covenant people and who had delivered them from slavery, was author and designer of all that is.

What Is God Like?

Then God *spoke*. The universe was created by a *word* (Genesis 1:3). Jews and Christians are not pantheists. We do not believe that God and the universe are one. We are not a part of the great universal Spirit, the way a drop of water is a part of an ocean. No, a separateness exists between God and the created order. God spoke, and order came into being. God stands apart yet involved. God stays close, in contact with that creation.

Later, when Jesus Christ came, Christians understood that in him the Word had become a human being. "Word" became a synonym for Jesus Christ. John had Genesis 1:3 in mind when he wrote, "In the beginning was the Word, and the Word was with God, and the

Word was God. . . . Everything came into being through the Word. . . . What came into being through the Word was life" (John 1:1-14). By God's word the universe came into being. Later, that Word walked among us.

The apostle Paul also wanted people to know that the Word God spoke in Creation was the same Word God spoke on the cross. "Because all things were created by him: both in the heavens and on the earth, the things that are visible and the things that are invisible. . . . Because all the fullness of God was pleased to live in him, and he reconciled all things to himself through him—whether things on earth or in the heavens. He brought peace through the blood of his cross" (Colossians 1:16-20).Thus Christians have come to perceive the Creation story.

Creation

Genesis is a Greek word that means "beginning," "origin." The opening Creation account (Genesis 1:1–2:3) is a carefully worded poem of praise to God, containing the accumulated faith of the covenant people.

The second account (2:4-25), and the older of the two, is a very ancient story, told long ago around campfires, under a star-studded sky. It was recited by one generation to another for centuries before it was written down.

The Creation psalms are songs of worship that spanned the centuries and are as comfortable for us today as they were for ancient Israel. These psalms chant songs of beauty and order and wonder.

The Jews, who have lived with Genesis for a long time, are amazed that Christians want to literalize the poetry. To take the imagery of the "first day" or "second day" as twenty-four-hour periods or to look for the bones of Adam in Mesopotamia is to miss the essential point. Even to interpret the days as eons or ages, comparing them to certain geological time frames, is to turn a faith statement into a scientific text.

The symbol of seven days is a faith statement. It implies progressive creativity and careful order. In understanding "the first day," "the second day," and so on, we need to remember,

> "In your perspective a thousand years
>   are like yesterday past,
>   like a short period during the night watch"
>   (Psalm 90:4).

But more, seven days are poetic symbols to show form and to remind us to order our lives as God has ordered the universe.

Some people have trouble with science and the Bible. They either say the Bible is not true, or they separate their study of science from their faith as if God does not understand how mountains are formed or how babies are born. But have you wondered why so many scientists are women and men of faith?

Because they know how much they do not know, how many questions they cannot answer except by faith. They see that the Creation stories are statements of faith, not geology or biology. They know that in Creation God acted and is continually acting to create and to bring order.

The wise father or mother responds to the child's question, "Who made God?" by answering, "Nobody. That's who God is—the one who started it all, the one who made you and me and everything." Theologians can do no better. They say, with the Bible, that God created order and meaning and purpose out of utter chaos. In the beginning of God's creation, "God said, 'Let there be light'" (Genesis 1:3).

But what shall we think about this created universe? The biblical refrain gives us a hint: "God saw how good it was" (1:4, 10, 12, 18, 21, 25).

Some religions, such as gnosticism, have taught that the material world is evil. The spiritual or the soul is good; the physical or the body is bad. Not so in Judaism and Christianity. Everything God made—knee joints and sex organs, flying fish and monkeys, the law of gravity and the changing seasons—is called good.

Look at the power in the Creation accounts: In a simple phrase, Genesis 1:16 says, "God made the stars and two great lights," the sun to light the day, the moon to light the night, and the infinite galaxies of the heavens. God is a great God!

A believer once asked a rabbi, "Why did God give us this mighty poem of Creation?" The rabbi's answer? "To teach us to rest on the Sabbath." Why? Because God observed Sabbath, and that makes it sacred. When we stop our work, we remember that we are God's creatures and that God will take care of us even when we rest. The loving God wants us to trust, to relax, to enjoy. If we rested, wondered, and appreciated on one day in seven, we would understand Jesus' words, "Notice how the lilies in the field grow. They don't wear themselves out with work, and they don't spin cloth. But I say to you that even Solomon in all of his splendor wasn't dressed like one of these" (Matthew 6:28-29). What an antidote for our frenzied, everyday, business-as-usual world.

Not only does the classic poem of faith tell us we belong to God; it tells us much more: We are made "in God's own image" (Genesis 1:27). What do you suppose that means?

Stewards

"Then God said, 'Let us make humanity in our image to resemble us so that they may take charge of the fish of the sea, the birds in the sky, the livestock, all the earth, and all the crawling things on earth'" (Genesis 1:26).

In Genesis, men and women are cocreators with God and stewards for God. Our sexuality is part of God's creative goodness, pronounced good by God's word. So we are to "be fertile and multiply; fill the earth and master it" (1:28). From time to time a heresy appears in the church to make sexuality sinful or dirty or evil.

But "male and female God created them" (1:27). When persons become self-centered, that self-centeredness will affect sexual relations as well as everything else. But God's creation as such is pronounced good.

We are to be stewards of the entire universe. The biblical world was before pesticides and pollutants, but the understanding is there.

We are to keep the air clean.

We are to keep water pure.

We are to save the topsoil and replenish the forests and protect the animals. We have been given a trust to maintain the balance of nature.

Now consider the older of the two Creation stories (2:4-25). Here, the order of Creation is different from the other. But like the opening Creation account, this account is a story of faith. Notice the dramatic symbols.

What do you think is the meaning of God's forming "the human from the topsoil of the fertile land" (2:7)?

What do you think the Scripture means by continuing "and blew life's breath into his nostrils. The human came to life" (2:7)?

What do you suppose is the symbolic significance of "the tree of the knowledge of good and evil" (2:9)?

NOTES

MARKS OF DISCIPLESHIP

We are God's creatures. As Christian disciples, we know we belong to God. God has claim on us. How do you show in the way you live that you belong to God?

Clearly, the Creation stories give us responsibility for caring for the earth, for plants and animals, birds and fish, air and water. Read again Psalm 8:6-9. What are you doing right now to exercise this stewardship of all creation?

Describe your day of rest. How does it reflect a quiet trust in the great, good, and loving God who has created you and who will sustain you? How could you rest more creatively on your Sabbath?

IF YOU WANT TO KNOW MORE

Take a walk outdoors. Be aware of the sky, the trees, the water. Take time to watch and listen and feel. Try to see something you have never seen before. From time to time say, "Thank you, God."

NOTES

Mark of Discipleship
Disciples know they belong to God, that God has claim on them. They place themselves under the power and authority of Scripture.

13

"Because I know my wrongdoings,
my sin is always right in front of me.
I've sinned against you—you alone."
—Psalm 51:3-4

2 The Rebel People

OUR HUMAN CONDITION

Because we have the capacity to make choices, we see ourselves as self-sufficient. We become self-centered. And because we want no limits placed on us, we rebel against our Creator in our attempt to take control. Yet we know that there is turmoil in the world and in ourselves, but we don't know why.

ASSIGNMENT

In preparation, read thoughtfully these passages about sin. Try to become a character in the Genesis stories. Imagine yourself in the garden of Eden, on Noah's ark, or helping to build the tower of Babel. Notice that in Jeremiah the prophet grieves over the sins of a whole society. In Second Samuel the prophet Nathan throws a blinding spotlight on David's sin. Psalm 51 is a confession of sin that could be your own.

Pray daily before study:

"Come back to me and have mercy on me;
that's only right for those who love your
name" (Psalm 119:132).

Prayer concerns for the week:

Day 1 **Read Genesis 3–4** (the Fall, Cain and Abel).

Day 2 **Read Genesis 6:5–9:29** (Noah and the Flood).

Day 3 **Read Genesis 11:1-9** (the tower of Babel).

Day 4 **Read Jeremiah 8:18–9:11** (a lament for Judah and Jerusalem).

Day 5 **Read 2 Samuel 11:1–12:7** (David's sin and Nathan's reproof); **Psalm 51** (confession).

Day 6 **Read "The Bible Teaching" and the "Marks of Discipleship" and answer the questions.**

Day 7 **Rest, pray, and attend class.**

THE BIBLE TEACHING

When did you first rebel and demand your own way? You can't remember? It must have been early in your life. So it was with the human race. When ancient Hebrews asked, "How did sin come into the world?" an elder would begin to tell the story of the first man and the first woman and the serpent. When the story was over, the people would nod their heads knowingly, for they then understood something about themselves and about the human race. Or someone would ask, "Why can't people get along with one another?" And the elder would tell the story about the building of the great tower and how everybody wanted to make a name for themselves. Again the people would nod with understanding.

Sin with its many manifestations runs through the Bible from beginning to end. We will study this theme in relation to freedom, relationship, temptation, rebellion, alienation, wickedness, and grace. Sin is not merely a topic. Sin is the human condition.

Freedom

God breathed into men and women the power to think, to decide. This will, this divinely granted freedom, makes us different from rocks, plants, and animals. We have a will so that we can make choices. We are not totally determined by forces inside us or outside us. God wants children, not puppets.

When God said, "Don't eat from the tree of the knowledge of good and evil" (Genesis 2:17), God appealed to man and woman's freedom of choice. They would be held accountable.

Like Adam and Eve, we have choices to make and are held accountable by God. In what ways and for what are you being held accountable to God?

Relationship

Sin makes no sense apart from relationship. If there is no God, there is no sin. We might violate social customs or stumble over the natural order, but sin is an affront to someone. We get out of step with our Creator. Sin changes our relationships with other people. Sin scrambles our inner person so that we experience feelings such as shame and guilt. The man and the woman disobeyed God, so they hid. They broke the innocent relationship of love and trust.

Temptation

Some people say, "The devil made me do it." That attitude sidesteps responsibility. Yet we are pushed and pulled by sinister forces. Human experience testifies to a "whisper in the ear." The subtle serpent symbolizes an evil power that tempts us. Jesus was tempted (Matthew 4:1-11). Which one of us does not know the tug and nudge of temptation?

When you are tempted, what are the words the serpent speaks to you?

Rebellion

Deeper than any individual act of wrongdoing is the human tendency to rebel. From the beginning, people have tried to break out of divine boundaries, grab control of their own lives, and ignore what they knew to be right. Human beings, in selfish striving, seek to be independent of God. We dislike being limited. Pride sweeps over us. The ancient Greeks called it *hubris*, pride that offends the gods and leads to destruction. The story of the tower of Babel shows our desire to be self-sufficient. Paul said, "They traded God's truth for a lie, and they worshipped and served the creation instead of the creator" (Romans 1:25).

Rebellion includes disobedience (or transgression) and self-centeredness. We turn from God when we want to do things our way. The seven deadly sins listed in the Middle Ages—pride, greed, lust, anger, gluttony, envy, sloth—are called source sins because they are the fountainhead of sinning. But behind them is a willful, disobedient, self-centered rebellion. This rebellion is complete and universal:

"There is no righteous person, not even one.
There is no one who understands.
   There is no one who looks for God"
     (Romans 3:10-11; see Psalms 14:3; 53:3).

Alienation

The woman and the man lived in blissful innocence, naturally trusting and loving God. The earth was their paradise. In childlike wonder, they did not know there was such a thing as evil. But with their disobedience came knowledge of wrongdoing, shame, guilt, alienation. They immediately covered themselves and went into hiding.

David tried to hide his adulterous and murderous actions from the nation, and even from his own conscience, until the prophet Nathan beamed the spotlight of truth on his soul.

What are some signs of your anger, guilt, alienation? What do you do to hide your sins?

One way to hide is by rationalizing. The man in the garden said, "The woman you gave me, she gave me some fruit from the tree, and I ate" (Genesis 3:12). And the woman countered, "The snake tricked me, and I ate" (3:13). When have you found yourself rationalizing and blaming others?

Wickedness

From the rebellious heart, all sorts of wickedness spring. We can talk about the Ten Commandments, about racism or cheating on income tax, about the drug traffic or child abuse or pornography or backbiting and gossip. From the brackish well of self-centeredness comes the foul water of our personal and collective sins. Cain's murder of Abel followed the parents' disobedience. Things went from bad to worse as Lamech cried out proudly, "I killed a man for wounding me, a boy for striking me" (Genesis 4:23).

The disease is widespread. The whole human race is infected.

Grace

With evil so pervasive, sin so vile, we wonder why God does not destroy us all. The Bible speaks of God's temptation to do so (Genesis 6:5-7). But there is always a restraining side to the action: Through Noah and his family, God gave humankind a chance to start again.

Notice, particularly in Genesis 3 and 4, the touch of God's grace even amid human rebellion. God did not abandon the woman and the man. God came to them, questioned them, but did not destroy them. Their punishment was a form of grace: The man would earn bread by sweat; yet work is one of life's great blessings. The woman would bear children with pain; yet children are usually so welcome that the pangs of childbirth are soon forgotten.

Did God lie when he said they would die? Did the serpent tell the truth when he said they would not? Both God and the serpent told their own truth. Life to God meant fulfillment, joy, a relationship of unblemished love. Life to the serpent meant eating and sleeping and going through the motions of living. When the woman and the man rebelled, something beautiful died. Innocence was destroyed. A relationship was broken. Pure love of God and one another was violated, mixed forever with guilt and spiritual separation. Cherubim and a flaming sword guard the garden of innocence. We can never go home again.

Yet God did not abandon the people. Even as God drove woman and man out of the land of innocence, God took the time and tenderness to make clothes for them and help them dress themselves (3:21). Notice also that the "sign on Cain" (4:15) was to protect him, not to persecute him as is commonly thought. The grace of God permeates the Bible. God's mercy accompanies people even in their wickedness. That grace culminates in the cross of Jesus Christ.

MARKS OF DISCIPLESHIP

As disciples, we acknowledge our human rebellion, accept our personal responsibility for sin, and repent, placing ourselves back under the authority of God.

We all try to hide our sinfulness, even from ourselves. Recall a time when some person or some event caused you to see your sinful nature.

Mark of Discipleship
Disciples acknowledge their rebellion, accept responsibility for their sin, and repent.

Because we tend to defy God and take life into our own hands, how do we go about putting ourselves back under God's authority? Read again Psalm 51.

We are part of the collective wickedness of the world. We have the capability of destroying ourselves. What, in your view, are the means and our chances of our survival?

IF YOU WANT TO KNOW MORE

Write a brief autobiography with your own "Adam and Eve" or "tower of Babel" story.

"I will make of you a great nation and will bless you. I will make your name respected, and you will be a blessing. . . . All the families of the earth will be blessed because of you."
—Genesis 12:2-3

3 The Called People

OUR HUMAN CONDITION

We are bewildered, overwhelmed. We search for a way to make sense out of life. We don't know what to do. We don't know how to begin. We yearn for a call that will take us beyond ourselves.

ASSIGNMENT

In preparation, read in great sweeps the ancestral sagas of the Bible: Abraham and Sarah; Isaac and Rebekah; Jacob, Rachel, Leah, and Jacob's twelve sons from whom descended the twelve tribes of Israel; and Joseph, the great provider. Read rapidly, being concerned not about detail but about gaining a sense of history, a feeling for a people called for a special mission.

Pray daily before study:

"You, LORD my God!
    You've done so many things—
    your wonderful deeds and your plans
        for us—
    no one can compare with you!
If I were to proclaim and talk about all of
        them,
    they would be too numerous to count!"
                (Psalm 40:5).

Prayer concerns for the week:

Day 1 **Read Genesis 12–13; 14:17–17:27** (call of Abram, covenant with God).

Day 2 **Read Genesis 18–23** (birth of Isaac, testing of Abraham).

Day 3 **Read Genesis 24–27** (Isaac and Rebekah).

Day 4 **Read Genesis 28–33; 35** (Jacob, Rachel, Leah, and the twelve sons).

Day 5 **Read Genesis 37; 39–41** (Joseph in Egypt); **42–45** (Joseph's brothers in Egypt); **47–50** (Jacob's move to Egypt).

Day 6 Read **"The Bible Teaching"** and the **"Marks of Discipleship"** and answer the **questions.**

Day 7 **Rest, pray, and attend class.**

THE BIBLE TEACHING

Picture the Near Eastern world in the second millennium B.C. In Egypt people worshiped the sun and Pharaoh. In Canaan the Canaanites worshiped on the high places, celebrating fertility with ritual prostitution and worship of weather gods. Peoples of Mesopotamia, including the Amorites, also a highly developed people, served many gods.

Into this world God called a people. God's purpose was to reveal the one true God, Creator of all that is, and to show a way of life compatible with God's holiness and helpful for human wholeness.

Read carefully Genesis 12:1-3. God wants a people who trust, a people who will leave their familiar surroundings (gods, culture, land) and go forth in obedience to a fresh place in order to be a blessing to all the families of the earth. As an integral part of this call, God will multiply Abram and Sarai into a great nation with a land of their own.

Covenant

Covenant is not contract. *Contract* is an agreement worked out between two parties. *Covenant* means a binding pact between God and God's people. God initiates covenant and stipulates all the provisions. People have the choice of accepting or rejecting it, but not of offering alternative plans or conditions. Blessing comes from trust and obedience.

The hinge verse is "Abram left just as the LORD told him" (Genesis 12:4). On that verse hangs the history of Israel. No wonder the Jews refer to "our father Abraham." The Muslims call him "friend of God," and Christians honor him as the father of the faithful.

Abram and Sarai left the Tigris and Euphrates Rivers that had rocked the cradle of civilization. (Their names were later changed to Abraham and Sarah. See 17:5, 15-16.) Early peoples in Mesopotamia had invented writing and the wheel, designed cities, initiated governments, and established an organized religion of moon god and fertility rites. But Abram and Sarai were called to become nomads in the rough and rugged terrain of Canaan.

God does not reveal God's will to the curious but to the obedient. Faith is not belief without proof; faith is obedience without reservation.

But what a foolish choice God made! Abram was seventy-five years old when he left Haran (12:4). God wanted to procreate a great people, and Abram was an old man. His wife Sarai was beyond the age of bearing children and barren as well. No wonder she laughed (18:12). Here we get a clue that God picks unlikely candidates to carry the colors: Moses, a stammerer to speak the law; Rahab, a prostitute to make a way into the Promised Land; David, a shepherd boy to be king; Jesus, a Jewish carpenter to be the Savior of the world. The Bible says God purposely chooses "what the world considers foolish to shame the wise" (1 Corinthians 1:27).

Consider for a moment some surprising (by worldly standards), even limited, people whom God has used in a mighty way. Jot down their names.

What weaknesses do you have that God might see as strengths and use?

Melchizedek, a priest of God Most High, seems to drop right out of heaven, bringing bread and wine (Genesis 14:18). No wonder early Christians saw him as a forerunner of Jesus, the great High Priest of God (Hebrews 6:19–7:3).

Melchizedek entered the picture centuries before the Levitical priesthood was formed. Abram took the bread and wine and gave a tithe to Melchizedek (Genesis 14:18-20).

The tithe became an essential part of worship for the covenant people. Old and New Testaments emphasize the tithe as a standard of faithful worship. Read what the prophet Malachi said about the tithe (Malachi 3:6-12). Jesus, interested in exuberant and sacrificial giving and stressing mercy and justice, nevertheless affirmed the practice of tithing (Matthew 23:23). The tithe emphasizes first fruits, proportionate giving (ten percent), regular offerings, and joyous worship. The tithe is a mark of discipleship for the people of God.

Sign of the Covenant

Circumcision was a sign of belonging to the covenant people (Genesis 17:9-14). No one can understand biblical history without understanding that Jewish males since the time of Abraham have been circumcised as the sign of belonging to the covenant people. Later, the religious leaders would call for and promise a circumcision of the heart (Deuteronomy 10:16; 30:6), recognizing that the physical symbol was not enough. Paul argued that Christians, if their hearts are filled with Jesus' spirit, do not need physical circumcision in order to belong to the followers of Christ (Galatians 5:6; 6:15). But among the Jews, circumcision is the sign of belonging to the people of God—Abraham, Isaac, and Jacob.

At times when the continuity of the covenant could have been broken, God acted in strong ways. Consider God's action:

The Testing of Abraham

God wanted to test Abraham's faith. God wanted him to be willing to offer up Isaac, the child of promise, Abraham's future. (Sometimes worshipers of Canaanite gods did offer their firstborn sons.) But God intervened, providing Abraham a ram as a substitute for his son. Light came to the whole world that God did not want child sacrifice. (See also Leviticus 18:21.) Even more important, Abraham was willing to put both his future and the significance of his life into the hands of God—proof of true worship. Abraham passed God's test; he proved faithful.

How willing are you to commit your future and the meaning and significance of your life to God?

Reaffirmation by Isaac

If Isaac had gone back to Mesopotamia, or if he had married a Canaanite woman, then all would have been lost. The arrangement of Isaac's marriage was essential to the continuity of the covenant (Genesis 24). Notice how the servant saw God's hand in the whole affair.

Later Isaac carried on the tradition and faith of his father. Look at this powerful symbol: "Isaac dug out again the wells that were dug during the lifetime of his father Abraham" (26:18). Then his servants dug his own well, "Well of giving one's word," showing his own personal commitment to the call of God (26:25, 32-33, footnote).

In what ways is your faith commitment a continuing of an important tradition?

Esau and Jacob

God can do more with a rascal than with a fool. Jacob was a conniving, cheating scoundrel. But he did care about the covenant. His name literally meant "heel grabber." His older twin Esau, as firstborn, should have carried on the covenant. But he was more concerned about hunting and fishing and eating. God went to work on Jacob, an unlikely prospect.

When Jacob was running for his life, God met him in a dream. When we sing, "We are climbing Jacob's ladder," we remember the angels ascending and descending. Jacob named the place Bethel, meaning "House of God." Notice that he confirmed his meeting with the God of Abraham and Isaac by pledging the tithe (Genesis 28:22).

Yet the rascal was not really changed until he was on his return journey to the homeland, the land of promise. Genesis 32:22–33:20 portrays one of the great wrestling matches of history and one of the Bible's most beautiful reconciliations. If you have ever wrestled all night with God and been blessed, then you, like Jacob, have a new name, Israel (meaning "one who struggles with God"), and you too will never be the same.

The two brothers were reconciled when Jacob limped up the hill, bowing low, and Esau ran to meet him, threw his arms around him, and kissed him (33:4). The reconciliation was cemented at the death of their father. These are precious words: "Isaac took his last breath and died. He was buried with his ancestors after a long, satisfying life. His sons Esau and Jacob buried him" (35:29).

Consider your own family relationships. Do you need to wrestle with God so you can "go home again"?

Joseph the Provider

Four sets of half brothers, a blended family conceived in bitterness because of jealousy among the mothers, a younger brother doted on by his father because he was born when his father was old—no wonder the other sons felt anger toward the favored one. But years later, long after the brothers had thrown Joseph into the pit, after Potiphar's prison, after dreams and harvests and famine, Joseph looked back over his life. He expressed forgiveness and reconciliation in his exclaiming to his brothers, "You planned something bad for me, but God produced something good from it" (Genesis 50:20). What an awareness of the strange providence of God!

In looking back over your life, where do you see God's shaping and guiding providence?

Recall an experience in your life when God made good come out of evil.

So the covenant community is called, shaped, tested, watched over by God. Imperfect people—doubting, conniving, arrogant people—are molded into a message: God is God of all creation. God is to be obeyed; children are to be respected; brothers are to be reconciled; food is to be shared; elderly are to be honored; God can be trusted. The light is beginning to shine for the whole world to see. And we are beginning to sense there is meaning to life, a direction to travel, a people of faith to whom we can belong. We are beginning to know what to do and whom to trust.

MARKS OF DISCIPLESHIP

The disciple responds to God's call to enter the covenant community of faith.

What are some marks by which we Christians can tell we are a part of God's community of faith?

Mark of Discipleship
Disciples respond to God's call to enter the covenant community of faith and express commitment to the covenant through the tithe.

What evidences of obedience and trust identify your commitment?

The tithe is one response to God's call that helps persons reach beyond themselves. Do you tithe? What are your reasons?

If not, are you willing to tithe during the remainder of this study, linking yourself more firmly to the covenant community of faith?

So much emphasis in contemporary Christianity is personal and individualistic. What helps you feel a sense of belonging to the called corporate people of God?

IF YOU WANT TO KNOW MORE

The theme of covenant runs throughout the Bible. In Genesis the covenant pattern generally is that of an agreement imposed by a greater power (God) on a lesser power (human beings). God states the requirements and expects human beings to comply with them. Such covenants often include a sign, or mark, to seal the agreement. Look for these biblical statements of covenant in Genesis, their signs, and the repeated phrase *enduring covenant*:

- Noah (all creation), 9:8-17
- Abraham, 12:2-3; 15:5, 17-21; 17:3-13, 21

For a fuller understanding of the various kinds of covenants in the Hebrew Scriptures, look up *covenant* in a Bible dictionary.

NOTES

> "I've clearly seen my people oppressed in Egypt. I've heard their cry of injustice because of their slave masters. I know about their pain. I've come down to rescue them from the Egyptians." —Exodus 3:7-8

4 God Hears the Cry

OUR HUMAN CONDITION

Human beings who are humiliated, exploited, or enslaved cry out for deliverance. They wait for a deliverer. They plead, "Does anybody care?"

ASSIGNMENT

Remember that the entire Old Testament is to be seen through "post-Exodus glasses" as the New Testament is to be viewed through "post-Resurrection glasses." The Israelites' understanding of who they were, who God is, and how God acted in history was shaped by the Exodus experiences. Those experiences influenced and shaped the life and faith of the Hebrew people in the same way the Resurrection influenced and shaped the life and faith of Christians.

Pray daily before study:

"Hear my words, LORD!
Consider my groans!
Pay attention to the sound of my cries,
my king and my God, because I am
praying to you!
LORD, in the morning you hear my voice.
In the morning I lay it all out before you.
Then I wait expectantly" (Psalm 5:1-3).

Prayer concerns for the week:

Day 1 **Read Exodus 1–4** (the oppression of the Hebrews and the call of Moses).

Day 2 **Read Exodus 5–7** (Moses confronting Pharaoh, beginning of the plagues).

Day 3 **Read Exodus 8–11** (remaining plagues).

Day 4 **Read Exodus 12–14** (explanation of Passover, death of the firstborn, escape from Egypt).

Day 5 **Read Exodus 15–18** (song of Moses, experiences in the wilderness); **Psalm 105** (thanksgiving for God's faithfulness to the covenant with Israel).

Day 6 **Read "The Bible Teaching" and the "Marks of Discipleship" and answer the questions.**

Day 7 **Rest, pray, and attend class.**

THE BIBLE TEACHING

Four hundred thirty years had passed since Joseph stored grain for Pharaoh, the king of Egypt. The Israelites had prospered on the good land called Goshen on the Nile Delta in northeastern Egypt. The descendants of Jacob's twelve sons had become, as God had promised Abraham, "as many as . . . the grains of sand on the seashore" (Genesis 22:17). By the time of Moses they numbered in the hundreds of thousands.

But the politics of Egypt took a downward turn for the Israelites. "Now a new king came to power in Egypt who didn't know Joseph" (Exodus 1:8). The Israelites were seen as an alien people who lived on the border and did not worship Egyptian gods. They were perceived as a threat because they were so numerous.

The powerful central government of the Nineteenth Dynasty of Egypt developed strong armies and constructed huge buildings. The Egyptian pharaohs Seti I and Rameses II built gigantic tombs and temples with mammoth statues. In the Nile Delta, they constructed the great storage cities of Pithom and Rameses. Israelite men as well as Egyptian peasants were forced into day labor. The work was hard, and the conditions oppressive. Slowly the kings turned the economic screw tighter and tighter. The Israelites became slaves, but they were so many in number that those in power began to fear them. Human life was cheap.

The king, with a paranoid mentality, decided to kill the Hebrew baby boys. First he appealed to the midwives, Shiphrah and Puah; and when that ploy did not work, he demanded that the baby boys be thrown into the Nile. Wailing was heard in the streets. Daily life was reduced to subhuman existence. Freedom gradually slipped away. The Hebrews were intimidated, resigned, helpless. The promises God had made to Abraham seemed far away and long ago.

Then one woman resisted. Moses' mother, Jochebed, slipped her baby into the Nile as Pharaoh commanded, but in a tar-covered basket. Moses' sister, Miriam, watched from a distance. The princess, Pharaoh's daughter, drew the baby out, and at the suggestion of Miriam hired a Hebrew woman, not knowing the woman was Moses' mother, to nurse him. The princess adopted Moses as her own son.

The name *Moses* carried two meanings. It is similar to the Egyptian word for "child" or "son," a son for the princess. But Israel understood "son" to stand for God's people. "Out of Egypt I called my son" (Hosea 11:1). *Moses* in Hebrew meant "drawn forth." He was drawn forth from the water, but later he drew forth the people through the water.

The boy was nurtured on his mother's Hebrew faith, listening to the lullabies of Israel. He was trained in the ways of the Egyptian king's court, educated by the finest scholars in the known world. Yet, when God said to Moses, "What is that in your hand?" Moses saw only a staff that stood as a symbol of himself—a Hebrew slave raised as an Egyptian, a runaway murderer, a stammerer living in the desert as a shepherd. But God saw a different man—a compassionate man who had drunk in the stories of Abraham and Sarah, Isaac and Rebekah, and Jacob and Rachel along with his mother's milk, and who had sharpened his mind on the mathematics and astronomy of the pyramids.

Moses had empathy for the oppressed. He was furious when an Egyptian beat a Hebrew (Exodus 2:11-12), offended when a Hebrew struck another (2:13), and quick to drive away troublemakers from Jethro's daughters (2:17).

When Moses took off his shoes and threw down his staff, he was ready to listen to God.

At first Moses objected to the call. The impossibility of the task seemed clear to him. He said in effect, "Bring it to pass, Lord, but not through me."

"I Am Who I Am"

Moses needed to know who was summoning him. Like Jacob wrestling with God at Jabbok, Moses demanded to know. "Tell me your name." Usually it was thought that to know someone's name was to have power over that person. Hence, most pagan gods did not reveal their names. God's revelation was cloaked in mystery. God's name both revealed and hid. Learning God's name still kept Moses in awe and under authority. The name can be translated "I Am" or "I Am Who I Am" or "I Will Be What I Will Be." Tell the people, said God, that "I Am" has sent you. Not the fertility gods of the Nile or of the high places of Canaan, not the sun god of Egypt or the moon god of Mesopotamia, but the God of Israel—the same who created the stars and the seas, the same who breathed life into men and women, the one who inspired your mother to place you in a basket and a compassionate woman to draw you from the water. I am "the God of your father, Abraham's God, Isaac's God, and Jacob's God." God reminded Moses of the history and character of the God who was talking to him. "I Am" has sent you.

Confronting Pharaoh

Moses asked Pharaoh's permission for the Israelites to make a three-day journey into the wilderness to make sacrifices to God. Pharaoh rightly suspected the Israelites would never return, so he refused the request.

Moses and Aaron, struggling with Pharaoh, performed signs and wonders as persuasion; but Pharaoh's magicians countered. Then the struggle began in earnest. Faith wrestled with unfaith; freedom fought against bondage. Ten plagues occurred—plagues not unknown to Egypt but occurring with severity, rapidity, and preannounced by Moses: pollution of the Nile, frogs, gnats, flies, livestock disease, boils, thunderstorms with hail, locusts, thick darkness, and finally death of the firstborn. Until the last plague, Pharaoh refused to let the people go.

In Exodus 4:21, we read that God had warned Moses that Pharaoh would not listen, that God would "make him stubborn." What does this mean? It means that willful resistance to God's

DISCIPLE FAST TRACK

intentions makes a person calloused. God allows us to resist God's word. When we make that choice, it is the beginning of a heart closed to God. Pharaoh's heart became stubborn and hard.

Hundreds of years later the prophet Isaiah described the same frame of mind in the people of Israel:

> "Make the minds of this people dull.
>   Make their ears deaf and their eyes blind,
>   so they can't see with their eyes,
>   or hear with their ears,
>   or understand with their minds,
>   and turn, and be healed" (Isaiah 6:10).

Jesus used this passage from Isaiah to describe the same condition in his time (Matthew 13:13-15; Mark 8:17-18). A resisting heart, as it continues to encounter the Word of God, becomes even more resistant.

The first wonders failed to impress the Egyptians. Their magicians could stiffen snakes, turn water blood red, and bring frogs out onto the land. But the plague of the gnats confounded them. "This is something only God could do!" they said (Exodus 8:19). Still Pharaoh refused to let the people go.

In reading the Bible narrative about Moses, remember the stories have interwoven traditions. Therefore, names for persons and for God, as well as accounts of particular events, may vary depending on which oral or written tradition they came from. For example, Reuel is the same person as Jethro; Horeb is the same as Sinai. Two traditions use a different word for the deity. One group of Hebrew writers used *Elohim* (God), and another used *Yahweh* (Lord). The distinction is blurred by the English translation.

Passover is often misunderstood. The Passover is not "passing over" the sea. Rather, Passover is the plague of death "passing over" or "sparing" the homes of the Israelites because they had obeyed God and anointed their doorposts with the lamb's sacrificial blood. (Imagine the forceful symbolism this event provides later for Christians!)

If you attend a Passover meal (Seder) with contemporary Jewish people, you eat the unleavened bread (the Israelites had to leave in a hurry and had no time for bread to rise), roasted lamb (remembering anointing of blood to obtain release and the quick feast in hope of freedom), and the bitter herbs dipped in salt water (remembering the bitter oppression and the tears of slavery).

Freedom Costs

Bondage carries a cost, but so does freedom. Most people do not realize the price of justice and freedom. Great leaders, however, do. Write down names of leaders who have led their people to freedom at great cost.

NOTES

People don't always react with joy when they are being delivered from bondage. Moses had great difficulty with the Israelites. They were often afraid, sometimes angry, and many times ready to abandon their dreams. When Moses and Aaron first proposed a three-day journey for a sacrificial feast, Pharaoh lashed back with his famous bricks-without-straw speech. The Israelite supervisors turned on Moses and Aaron, accusing them of making their slavery even more painful (Exodus 5:15-21).

Recall a time when justice was needed, when power struck down hard, and people blamed their own leaders:

Fear of the unknown and anxiety about their future caused the Israelites to complain again and again. After the plagues, as they stood on the brink of freedom, they panicked. The sea was before them, the chariots behind them. They cried out, "Weren't there enough graves in Egypt that you took us away to die in the desert?" (14:11). How human! Once again Moses spoke the word of faith: "Don't be afraid. Stand your ground, and watch the LORD rescue you today" (14:13).

When they complained about food, God provided quail and then manna (16:13-15). To this day, quail migrate across the Mediterranean Sea and drop exhausted in the desert. The manna was a flaky, sweet substance gathered early in the morning to be ground and made into bread. The people were to gather enough manna for one day except on the sixth day. Then they were to gather enough to have some left over for the Sabbath (16:22-26). Notice that the writer of Exodus constantly reinforces the importance of the Sabbath.

The message of Exodus is God hears, God sees, God knows, God remembers, and God acts. That theme is chanted liturgically in Deuteronomy 6:21-25; 26:5-10; and Joshua 24:2-14, as well as remembered by the prophets (Hosea 11:1-4). It states the salvation experience of the Israelites.

God's action in the Exodus has eternal and universal implications. When the social systems of humankind become oppressive, God hears the cry of the oppressed and acts.

God's covenant with Abraham and his descendants is still valid. God is faithful to the agreement. In the Exodus, God fulfills the promise of deliverance. That promise is to everyone who is "in Egypt," to everyone who is in bondage.

DISCIPLE FAST TRACK

MARKS OF DISCIPLESHIP

Weaving its way through the Exodus story (and at times rising above the story itself) is the strong, assuring message that God is faithful to God's promise. God's covenant stands!

God hears the cries of those in bondage and calls them into freedom. The faithful disciple hears and obeys God's call to be a bearer of God's message of deliverance.

The Israelites were caught in an oppressive social system. They were trapped politically and economically. Think about people today who are caught in oppressive social systems. How do such systems come into being? How can we change them?

Those who have been in bondage individually or as a people have a deliverance story to tell. Tell a deliverance story.

How does personal deliverance from bondage differ from the deliverance of the Israelites from slavery?

Have you ever felt that you had too much power over other persons? Or that other persons had too much power over you? Describe the situation.

Mark of Discipleship
Disciples hear and obey God's call to be bearers of God's message of deliverance.

The call of Moses is central to Exodus. Describe any times in your life when you have felt God speaking to or calling you.

Describe any sense of reluctance you have felt about responding when God called you to a difficult task.

In the Passover Haggadah, a Jewish liturgy for Seder, it is written, "I am a Jew because in every place where suffering weeps, the Jew weeps. I am a Jew because every time when despair cries out, the Jew hopes."

Christians have been grafted into Abraham's people (Romans 11:17-19), and our roots are in the people Israel. So Exodus is our history too. What is it about being Christian that causes us to weep with the suffering and hope with the despairing?

IF YOU WANT TO KNOW MORE

See what you can discover about the building programs during the time of Seti I and Rameses II.

"Moses called out to all Israel, saying to them: 'Israel! Listen to the regulations and the case laws that I'm recounting in your hearing right now. Learn them and carefully do them.'" —Deuteronomy 5:1

5 God Sends the Law

OUR HUMAN CONDITION

We cannot abide chaos. We want structure. Boundaries give a sense of security. We need order to feel we belong.

ASSIGNMENT

Here we are studying the Law, and admittedly, it is slow going. In places you will want to read carefully, word for word, as in a law book. Later in this study, you will find references back to these laws.

Pray daily before study:

"LORD, teach me what your statutes
 are about,
 and I will guard every part of them.
Help me understand so I can guard your
 Instruction
 and keep it with all my heart.
Lead me on the trail of your
 commandments
 because that is what I want"
 (Psalm 119:33-35).

Prayer concerns for the week:

Day 1 **Read Exodus 19–20** (Israel at Sinai); **Deuteronomy 4:44–5:33** (summary of the Law). Compare.

Day 4 **Read Numbers 13:1–14:38** (spies sent to Canaan). **Deuteronomy 5; 6; 9** (what God requires). **Notice Deuteronomy 6:4-9** (this passage is called the Shema, which means "Hear").

Day 2 **Read Exodus 21:1–23:19** (laws concerning slaves, restitution, sabbath, and feasts); **31:18–32:35** (the golden calf).

Day 5 **Read Numbers 18** (priests and Levites); **Deuteronomy 14:22–15:23; 34** (tithe, sabbatical year, death of Moses).

Day 3 **Read Leviticus 11** (clean and unclean animals); **17:10–19:37** (sexual relations, the law of love).

Day 6 **Read "The Bible Teaching" and the "Marks of Discipleship" and answer the questions.**

Day 7 **Rest, pray, and attend class.**

THE BIBLE TEACHING

Law makes life tolerable. Without law, society explodes into fragments. Law keeps the strong from destroying the weak. Law lubricates social interaction. Law helps us know who we are. It reassures us that we belong to a given people. The Law helps to hold the covenant people together, to give some sense of social justice, and to provide the light of morality to the world.

Moses is called the lawgiver. Traditionally the first five books of the Bible, the Torah (Law) or Pentateuch (Five Scrolls), have been attributed to Moses. Torah is the heartbeat of Jewish religion. Certainly Moses began the law process with the Hebrew people in the wilderness. Can you imagine the task of creating a covenant community out of multitudes of newly freed slaves camping out in the wilderness? Torah was oral for centuries, modified, added to, and codified (arranged systematically), but probably not fixed in its present form until about 400 B.C. Traditions reflecting the rough nomadic wilderness experience and the later settled agricultural life were blended with traditions of Temple worship.

The highest spiritual exercise for Jews is Torah study:

"Instead of doing those things,
 these persons love the LORD's Instruction,
 and they recite God's Instruction day and night!"
(Psalm 1:2).

When the Torah scroll is removed from the holy ark during worship in synagogues today, the worshipers rise. When the Torah scroll is carried, those nearest to it kiss its embroidered mantle.

The Law made the people of Israel a distinct people. That was its purpose. Just as Israel's food laws separated the clean animals from the unclean, so Israel's people were a "separated" people. "I am the LORD who brought you up from the land of Egypt to be your God. You must be holy, because I am holy" (Leviticus 11:45).

Slowly the covenant people took form and identity. Circumcision became a sign of God's covenant with Abraham and of belonging to the covenant community. Sabbath, blessed of God in Creation, was honored as a holy and joyous day of rest. The Exodus experience of deliverance shaped the faith community forever. Then God added the most powerful cohesive force of all, the Law given to Moses.

The Law cannot be separated into religious and civil law. All aspects of life and society came under its rule. Still, we will look at different parts of it.

Laws of Social Welfare

When a parent "lays down the law" to a child, the child asks why. Our concern in studying the Mosaic law will be with the why.

"Don't mistreat or oppress an immigrant." Why? Because "you were once immigrants in the land of Egypt" (Exodus 22:21).

"Don't treat any widow or orphan badly" (22:22). Why? Because "you can be sure that I'll hear their cry" (22:23) as I heard your cries in Egypt.

"If you lend money to my people who are poor among you, don't be a creditor and charge them interest. If you take a piece of clothing from someone as a security deposit, you should return it before the sun goes down. His clothing may well be his only blanket to cover himself. What else will that person have to sleep in?" (22:25-27). Notice the reason, for this law goes beyond simple justice: "If he cries out to me, I'll listen, because I'm compassionate" (22:27).

Why be compassionate? Because you were once poor, you were once in bondage, you were once widows and orphans, you were once immigrants and tenants, you once cried out. Don't forget! The same God who heard your cry hears the cry of the poor now and says, "I'm compassionate."

When the Hebrews became farmers, the poor were permitted to glean behind the harvesters. The story of Ruth and Boaz found in the Book of Ruth is an account of a poor foreign-born widow who was allowed to pick up broken heads of barley from the fields. The "leavings" of figs or olives, after the pickers had finished, were for orphans and widows. This law made survival possible for the poor. Listen to Torah: "When you harvest your land's produce, you must not harvest all the way to the edge of your field; and don't gather up every remaining bit of your harvest. Also do not pick your vineyard clean or gather up all the grapes that have fallen there. Leave these items for the poor and the immigrant: I am the LORD your God" (Leviticus 19:9-10).

In a harsh, primitive world, what a light of compassion! Abraham and the covenant people were indeed blessed to be a blessing. What are some examples in our society of compassion providing for the poor, the immigrant, the orphan, and the widow?

Food Laws

Read again the food laws in Leviticus 11. Notice the following clean and unclean distinctions: land animals (11:2-8), aquatic animals (11:9-12), fowl (11:13-19), insects (11:20-23), and other food concerns (11:24-45). Just as important was the prohibition not to boil a goat in its mother's milk (Exodus 23:19; 34:26). That concern was so strong that in a kosher kitchen today, meat products and milk products are not cooked in the same vessels or served on the same plates. Eating blood was prohibited. Today the blood must be drained carefully from the meat, the meat soaked for half an hour, then covered with salt for an hour. In kosher meat the hip sinew is removed to recall how God touched Jacob's hip, causing him to limp.

Why these food restrictions? Many people have speculated on their healthful impact in a primitive culture long before modern knowledge of disease. Without doubt, abstaining from eating contaminated animals had a health factor; sanitation laws were a health breakthrough. Surely the inspired wisdom of Moses and the priests influenced the food laws to ensure health and well-being.

But from the biblical perspective, health factors were not the point at all. The Israelites were to be set apart, under special restrictions, deliberately different from other people. The point was not health; it was obedience. They were to be God's people, distinct. These restrictions were holy laws. You can see that table fellowship with non-Jews became extremely difficult. Before long, a Jew who ate with a Gentile violated covenant, spurned the holy faith, and was considered a sinner.

This study about food may seem unimportant to contemporary Christians; but it greatly affects our understanding of the New Testament, especially the experience of table fellowship among peoples.

Laws of Justice

Justice in early biblical times was often capricious, vindictive, arbitrary. Rulers could punish with a wave of the hand. Retribution between families or tribes often meant retaliating with double measure. In contrast, the law of Moses demanded uniformity and fairness. Witnesses were required; perjury was a grave offense. Judges were expected to be just. People in power were guided by the law that stood above them. The concept that no one is above the law is a biblical concept.

Later, when we read about King David or King Ahab, we will discover that when they thought they were above the law, the prophets brought them back into accountability.

Phrases such as *an eye for eye, and a tooth for tooth* seem severe to us now. But they were designed to stop the taking of a life in retribution for the loss of an eye and to stop the murder of a man who had knocked out a tooth. Recall that in Genesis Lamech bragged,

> "I killed a man for wounding me,
>   a boy for striking me;
> so Cain will be paid back seven times
>   and Lamech seventy-seven times" (Genesis 4:23-24).

Do you suppose this quotation was in Jesus' mind when he told Peter to forgive seventy-seven times?

Other laws insisted that false weights and measures are offensive to God. "You must have only one weight, complete and correct. . . . all who do business dishonestly . . . are detestable to the LORD your God" (Deuteronomy 25:15-16).

Later, the prophets of Israel would chastise the people for cheating, for lying, for using scales that were false and measurements that were unjust. Why? Because God is a just God. God wants fair dealings in the marketplace.

In your business dealings, can you think of any place where you are using "false weights and measures," where you falsify or mislead?

Give some examples of false and misleading advertising.

The law of Moses has a deep sense of fairness, of justice. Why? Because justice is grounded in the character of God. God is a just God.

Family Life

The Law builds in deep respect for parents. In the Ten Commandments, honor for father and mother preceded even the commandments on murder and adultery. The family was of utmost importance to the Hebrews.

"Anyone who violently hits their father or mother should be put to death" (Exodus 21:15). A capital offense! "Don't boil a young goat in its mother's milk" (23:19; 34:26) not only protested a Canaanite method of preparing a sacrifice but also reflected offense at a familylike insult.

Given the increasing conflict of demands within the family, how do you think adult children can faithfully honor their elderly parents?

What attitudes and actions toward your parents do your children hear and see from you?

Sexual relationships are heavily regulated by the law of Moses. Adultery carries a death penalty. Sex between persons of the same gender is prohibited. So are sexual relations with animals. Seduction of a virgin is a severe transgression, and punishment for rape can be as severe as for murder. Later you will notice that in the New Testament church adherence to many Jewish laws, such as food laws, was not required by the council at Jerusalem (Acts 15:19-20). But the requirement of sexual morality was upheld by all parties.

In a society where sexual promiscuity and adultery are rampant, what can you do to encourage faithfulness within marriage?

What can the church do?

MARKS OF DISCIPLESHIP

For the disciple, all the words of the law may be summed up in the commandment, "Love the LORD your God with all your heart, all your being, and all your strength" (Deuteronomy 6:5). "These words . . . must always be on your minds" (6:6). To keep these words is to *do* these words.

Mark of Discipleship
Disciples keep God's law by doing it.

Identify some of the words of the law that, through your obedience, bring order to your life.

. . . that bring security to your family.

. . . that give you a sense of belonging.

Try to recall times in your life when failure to obey God's law resulted in chaos.

IF YOU WANT TO KNOW MORE

Memorize the Ten Commandments.

The Law gives dignity to each person—to the poor, the immigrant, and the slave. Read Deuteronomy 24:10-13. Find other passages that give dignity to persons on the fringes of society.

> "A creature's life is in the blood. I have provided you the blood to make reconciliation for your lives on the altar, because the blood reconciles by means of the life."
> —Leviticus 17:11

6 When God Draws Near

OUR HUMAN CONDITION

When God draws near to us, we feel guilty and ashamed because of our sin. We are overwhelmed by our need of forgiveness when we are in the presence of God. What are we to do?

ASSIGNMENT

We are studying forms of ancient Hebrew worship. Pay particular attention to how the Hebrew people remembered their deliverance from slavery, how they were reconciled to God and one another, and how they gave thanks for what God had done.

Some elements in Christian worship including language and ritual have roots in the ancient Hebrew practices. As you read, watch for those roots.

Pray daily before study:

"I will fulfill my promises to you, God.
I will present thanksgiving offerings
to you" (Psalm 56:12).

Prayer concerns for the week:

Day 1   **Read Exodus 24–27** (covenant ratification, the ark of the covenant, the Tabernacle).

Day 2   **Read Exodus 34:29–36:1** (new tablets, offerings for the Tabernacle); **40** (glory of the Lord).

Day 3   **Read Leviticus 1–4:12; 5:1-6** (the burnt offering, offerings of well-being, sin and guilt offerings).

Day 4   **Read Leviticus 6–7** (ritual for offerings, the priests' portion); **Deuteronomy 18** (Levites).

Day 5   **Read Leviticus 16–17 in the New Revised Standard Version** (Day of Atonement); **Leviticus 23** (appointed festivals).

Day 6   **Read "The Bible Teaching" and the "Marks of Discipleship" and answer the questions.**

Day 7   **Rest, pray, and attend class.**

DISCIPLE FAST TRACK

THE BIBLE TEACHING

Why were the worship rules so complex and so specific? To us they seem ridiculous. But in that time, many worship practices of other peoples were offensive to the Lord. Such practices included witchcraft, astrology and magic, cult prostitution, and Baal worship on the high places. Other peoples worshiped the moon or sun or graven images. These practices were strictly forbidden to the Hebrews, for Israel belonged to God, totally and completely.

The people of Israel were trying to be a unified people, living under the rule of God. So the rules for worship and for all of life were intermingled. The people were tied to the soil; animals and crops were their life. Their worship flowed naturally from their daily existence. The work of their hands was represented in their sacrifices and worship.

Focus now on three aspects of early Hebrew worship:

Remembrance

The people of freedom can never forget their deliverance. The "passover" from Egypt symbolizes every experience of salvation, historical and personal. Celebration of Passover today is a family celebration, a remembrance designed for intimacy. That is why relatives and close friends are often included. Passover is especially designed to teach children. As we read in the Torah: "You should explain to your child on that day" (Exodus 13:8). Jews call the Passover ceremonial feast the Seder, which means order (of the meal or service). It is a serious but joyful observance. According to the Haggadah, the book read during the Passover Seder, this night is "different from all other nights."

Passover night is a time to remember
- that miraculous deliverance of the children of Israel in the face of impossible odds;
- divine sustenance (manna and quail);
- divine wisdom (the Law at Mount Sinai);
- freedom and the Promised Land.

The service ends not only in joy but in clarification: Worshipers understand what they have not known or have forgotten, what they have misunderstood or have neglected.

Jesus transformed the Passover meal for Christians. If the Last Supper was a Passover meal as supposed, the bread used by Jesus was matzah. In many Christian denominations the bread used for Holy Communion must be unleavened. The earliest Christians, who were Jews, associated the death of Jesus with the sacrifice of the Passover lamb. Jesus' sacrifice, which freed persons from slavery to sin, gave new meaning to the celebration of freedom from slavery.

The remembrance of deliverance from Egypt became the remembrance of deliverance from sin. Easter was originally called "the Pascha," from the Hebrew word *Pesach*, meaning "Passover." Sometimes Holy Communion is called the *Eucharist*, the feast of thanksgiving.

What are some of the remembrances you experience when eating the bread and drinking from the cup?

Atonement

Do you remember what we said about sin? Deeper than acts of wrongdoing, sin is broken relationships. God is offended. Barriers are erected. Guilt and shame come rushing in. Neighbor is alienated from neighbor. The human soul begins to fight a civil war within itself. In the Creation story, Adam and Eve hid from God. Today we often repress unresolved guilt, which results in emotional, mental, and social illness.

The ancient Israelites ritualized their expressions of guilt with carefully prescribed worship experiences. They confessed their sin and expressed their guilt and shame as a corporate community of faith. They made amends directly to the one who was offended— their Creator, Redeemer God.

Leviticus 16 helps us understand the Day of Atonement (Yom Kippur) and atonement sacrifices. (The Common English Bible calls this the Day of Reconciliation.) Once a year the chief priest (Aaron) cleansed himself, put on holy garments, and killed a bull as an offering. The blood sacrifice was a sin offering for himself and his house. Then Aaron chose two goats to bear symbolically the sins of the people. He offered one as a blood sacrifice for atonement. Aaron then laid both his hands on the head of the second goat, confessing "all the Israelites' offenses and all their rebellious sins, as well as all their other sins." He put their sins upon the head of the goat and sent the goat into the wilderness (Leviticus 16:21). The goat vicariously carried the sins away, freeing the people from their guilt and shame. Hence the name *scapegoat*.

Many teachers have explained atonement as "at-one-ment." Through atonement we are reconciled to God, made at one with God. We are freed to be in fellowship and no longer need carry the load of guilt.

Explain whether your church's rituals (and which rituals) are helping you feel freed of guilt and shame.

Explain whether your church's rituals (and which rituals) are helping you feel reconciled to God and neighbor.

DISCIPLE FAST TRACK

Thanksgiving

A significant element of Hebrew worship was the offering of gifts to God and God's acceptance of those gifts. Through the celebrative days prescribed in the festival calendar of the Law, the Hebrews relived the story of how their ancestors became bound to God in covenant and expressed their thanksgiving by offering gifts to God:

- New Year (Rosh Hashanah), also called festival of trumpets, in September–October at the beginning of the religious calendar.
- Day of Atonement (Yom Kippur) ten days later, the most solemn of all Jewish holy days, a day of penitence and fasting and purification of the sanctuary.
- Feast of Booths (Succoth), two weeks after the New Year and five days after Yom Kippur. In Leviticus 23:33-43 and Deuteronomy 16:13-15, the outline was clear: seven days of feasting and worship when the autumn harvest was over; a time of joy, thanksgiving, and celebration; no laborious work; and invitations to "the Levites, the immigrants, the orphans, and the widows who live in your cities" (16:14).
- Passover (Pesach), commemorating the Israelites' deliverance from slavery in Egypt, eight days in the spring that began with the Feast of Unleavened Bread and concluded with the offering of first fruits of the barley harvest.
- Pentecost (Shavuot, meaning "Weeks"), also called the Feast of Weeks because this feast fell on the fiftieth day after Passover (a week of weeks, or seven weeks, had passed), celebration of the offering of first fruits of the wheat harvest (waving the sheaf), the day of the Holy Spirit experience recorded in Acts 2.

Today most people have jobs unrelated to agriculture. How can we offer the fruit of our hands in worship and thanksgiving?

MARKS OF DISCIPLESHIP

When God draws near, it seems as if someone has turned on a light in the dirty, dusty rooms of our hearts. In the dark we pretended we were clean. In the light our failures stand out boldly. That is why we try to hide from God, lest truth and pure love find us out.

So in worship we not only discover God drawing near to us, but we find our lives inadequate. Close to God, we recognize that we are in need of prayer. Our need cries out. Our guilt pleads for forgiveness.

Mark of Discipleship
Disciples commit themselves to corporate worship.

The most striking characteristics of Hebrew worship are these:
- Worship is corporate.
- Worship is mandatory.
- Worship is prescribed.

So many Christians take worship lightly, worshiping occasionally as they feel like it. Others consider faith a private matter, as if their religion were solely between themselves and God. Still others find form, tradition, and ritual a restriction on their free spirits. But the habits and patterns of biblical worship are community based. Individual feelings, preferences, and subjective influences are not allowed to destroy the sacred traditions. Corporate worship teaches children, youth, and adults
- to remember,
- to ask for forgiveness, and
- to give thanks.

Christian disciples commit themselves to corporate worship for the same reasons. The Letter to the Hebrews in the New Testament draws heavily on atonement imagery: "We have confidence that we can enter the holy of holies by means of Jesus' blood, through a new and living way that he opened up for us through the curtain, which is his body, and we have a great high priest over God's house. Therefore, let's draw near with a genuine heart with the certainty that our faith gives us, since our hearts are sprinkled clean from an evil conscience and our bodies are washed with pure water. . . . Let us consider each other carefully for the purpose of sparking love and good deeds. Don't stop meeting together with other believers, which some people have gotten into the habit of doing. Instead, encourage each other, especially as you see the day drawing near" (Hebrews 10:19-25).

Disciples of Jesus should be drawn to communal worship with excitement and joy.

Describe your reaction to these words:

> "I rejoiced with those who said to me,
>   'Let's go to the LORD's house!' " (Psalm 122:1).

Do they ring true for you? Why?

In terms of worship, which element do you find most meaningful: remembrance, atonement, or thanksgiving? Why?

IF YOU WANT TO KNOW MORE

Do some research and write a paragraph on the levitical priesthood. Try to discover when in Israel's history animal sacrifice came to an end, and why.

"Then the LORD raised up leaders to rescue them [Israel] from the power of these raiders." —Judges 2:16

7   The People Without a King

OUR HUMAN CONDITION

We cannot tolerate political disorder and confusion. We swing between desiring unity born of faithfulness and wanting to "do our own thing." We need leadership. Please, somebody give us a sense of direction.

ASSIGNMENT

The Book of Joshua stresses what occurs when the people "trust and obey," when the leadership is faithful and the people are united.

The Book of Judges stresses what happens when the people do not "trust and obey," when they act individually rather than as a united community.

Pray daily before study:

"Rise up, God! Judge the earth
   because you hold all nations in your
      possession!" (Psalm 82:8).

Prayer concerns for the week:

Day 1 **Read Joshua 1–3** (Joshua's commission, Rahab and the spies, entering the land).

Day 2 **Read Joshua 4–6** (memorial stones, fall of Jericho); **24** (covenant at Shechem, death of Joshua).

Day 3 **Read Judges 1–2** (incomplete conquest, apostasy); **4** (Deborah).

Day 4 **Read Judges 6–8** (Gideon).

Day 5 **Read Judges 13–16** (Samson).

Day 6 **Read "The Bible Teaching" and the "Marks of Discipleship" and answer the questions.**

Day 7 **Rest, pray, and attend class.**

DISCIPLE FAST TRACK

THE BIBLE TEACHING

The Book of Joshua is transitional. The return to Canaan fulfills the promise of land made to Abraham and Sarah. Joshua, as Moses' successor, completes the saga of faith: Trust God's promises, and God will bring victory.

In some ways the book should be tied to the Pentateuch (Law), the first five books of the Bible. It is stamped with the style of Deuteronomy; that is, it stresses obedience to the covenant. But Jewish scholars who compiled the canon (the official books of the Hebrew Scriptures) placed Joshua with the judges, the kings, and the prophets. Yet Joshua was not exactly a judge either, not like Gideon or Deborah. So we use the term *transitional* because Joshua came between the time of Moses and the time of the judges, between the time of the Exodus and the time of tribal government under the judges.

Joshua completed Moses' work of deliverance. In faithfulness to God, he led the people into the land of promise. The name *Joshua* means "Yahweh is salvation" or "salvation" and has the same Hebrew root as the name *Jesus*.

Remember the twelve spies? Joshua and Caleb saw the land of "milk and honey" and wanted to go up and possess it (Numbers 13:25–14:38), but they lost by a vote of ten to two. Now, after forty years of wilderness wandering, the generation of pessimists has died, the people have been tempered by years of desert discipline, and Moses is buried. Joshua, God's faithful leader, takes up Moses' mantle and crosses the Jordan. Notice the parallels between Moses and Joshua:

Moses	Joshua
Spies to Hebron area (Numbers 13)	Spies to Jericho area (Joshua 2)
Crossing the Red Sea (Exodus 14)	Crossing the Jordan (Joshua 3)
Circumcision (Exodus 4:24-26)	Circumcision again (Joshua 5:2-7)
Passover (Exodus 12:1-36)	Observe Passover (Joshua 5:10)
"Take off your sandals," burning bush (Exodus 3:1-5)	"Take your sandals off," man with drawn sword (Joshua 5:13-15)
The gesture of strength, "Moses held up his hand" (Exodus 17:8-13)	"Point the dagger in your hand" (Joshua 8:18-21)
Law given at Mount Sinai (Shechem) (Exodus 24)	Law written again on stone at Mount Ebal (Shechem) (Joshua 8:30-35)
Cities of refuge, anticipated by Moses (Numbers 35:9-15)	Cities of refuge, appointed and named (Joshua 20)
Covenant at Sinai (Exodus 24:7-8)	Covenant at Shechem (Joshua 24:15, 24-25)

NOTES

NOTES

Writers of biblical history used the elements of conquest to affirm Israel's faith. Just as God had delivered Israel from slavery, so God had led the people into the land of promise.

Looking back on Joshua and his time, Israel understood the meanings hidden in the dramatic and often bloody events: God fought for Israel. The constant theme was "out of Egypt . . . into the land of promise." The continual assumption, using various stories and strains of history, was that to violate the covenant meant chaos in the life of the people; to keep the covenant was to fulfill Israel's purpose with order and meaning.

Joshua's words ring clear:

"If it seems wrong in your opinion to serve the LORD,
then choose today whom you will serve. . . . But my family
and I will serve the LORD" (Joshua 24:15).

Judges

Many of the judges were not what we think of as judges. Perhaps a better description would be "charismatic leaders." All were tribal leaders—men and women who were raised up by the Lord in time of crisis and confusion to call Israel back to obedience, to unify the people, and to lead them in battle against an assortment of enemies. "The LORD raised up leaders to rescue them from the power of these raiders" (Judges 2:16).

Deborah, Gideon, and Samson were three of those called by God to be judges. They served for a time, and when their task was accomplished, they disappeared. They were not noted for their great spiritual qualities but for their willingness to hear and respond to the call of God. They were not so much heroes as they were instruments of the Lord.

The Israelites, under the leadership of Moses and Joshua, were a theocracy, governed by the direct authority of God. As they settled down in Canaan, they functioned as tribes in a loosely knit confederacy. No president, no pharaoh, no king ruled them. The spiritual leaders wanted God to be their king. Gideon said, "I'm not the one who will rule over you, and my son won't rule over you either. The LORD rules over you" (Judges 8:23). Until the time of the kings, the leaders were religious and military leaders who served for a short time.

Psalm 24 identifies God as Israel's King:

"Mighty gates: lift up your heads!
   Ancient doors: rise up high!
      So the glorious king can enter!
Who is this glorious king?
   The LORD, strong and powerful!
   The LORD, powerful in battle!" (Psalm 24:7-8).

Later on, Israel would demand a king. Their enemies would seem better organized, more unified, better equipped for war. Samuel would waver, warn the people about potential taxes, conscripted labor for war and construction of palaces, political pomp and pride, and military authority. But finally he would yield to their wishes.

But during the two-hundred-year period of the judges, from the time of Joshua's death until the rise of the monarchy (King Saul), various judges insisted that the Lord was Israel's true ruler. Imagine farmers and herdsmen, people under periodic attack and conflict, trying to maintain their land, herds, and family and tribal life without a central government.

During these conflicts they were continually influenced by pagan Canaanite religious practices. Thus we read in Judges of frequent apostasy (abandonment of faith), divine disapproval, urgent appeals to God in time of crisis, and the raising up of leaders to throw off oppressors. After the victories, they returned to their family lands and to peace again. But the chaos eventually returned. The recurring pattern during the period of the judges was apostasy, punishment, penitence, and peace.

Now consider as examples these judges:

Deborah

Picture the situation: Jabin had "oppressed the Israelites cruelly for twenty years" (Judges 4:3). His general Sisera commanded nine hundred iron chariots. The Canaanites had a tremendous military advantage because their iron weapons were vastly superior to the Israelite weapons. The Israelites were frightened, incapable of united action, and lacked the courage to face the enemy.

Enter two women: Deborah (the name means "bee") and Jael (the name means "mountain goat"). Deborah was a prophet and judge, and Jael a Kenite. Barak, the Israelite general, pleaded with Deborah, "If you'll go with me, I'll go; but if not, I won't go" (4:8). She replied, "The path you are taking won't bring honor to you, because the LORD will hand over Sisera to a woman" (4:9).

With great faith, Deborah said to Barak, "Hasn't the LORD gone out before you?" (4:14). She chose for the battle the Valley of Jezreel, seemingly perfect for maneuverability of the enemy chariots. The Israelites waited on Mount Tabor.

Then "the sky poured down" (5:4). The river Kishon flooded the plain, and the chariots became stuck in the mud. (Remember the Egyptian chariots that also got stuck in the mud?) Israel won a great victory.

The defeated general Sisera found refuge in the tent of Jael, a non-Israelite woman. While Sisera slept, Jael drove a tent spike through his head. The mighty chariots of iron were defeated by a "bee," a "mountain goat," some mud, and God. Now, there would be forty years of peace.

Gideon

Once again "the Israelites did things that the LORD saw as evil" (Judges 6:1). Israel was in disarray. The Midianites raided them continually. All around them Canaanite peoples practiced Baal worship. Baalim were fertility gods whose worship on the "high places" (hill shrines) the Bible condemns. The Israelites continually intermingled their worship with these neighborhood fertility religions. Prophets and judges condemned Baal worship because it involved sexual orgies, including both male and female sacred prostitutes; human sacrifice; drunkenness; and worship of animal images, sexual organs, trees, and other idols.

Now the Lord called Gideon.

Where was he? In a wine press, separating wheat from chaff! Why wasn't he out in the open where the wind could blow the chaff away? Because he was hiding from the Midianites; he was afraid. Notice the irony when the angel of the Lord said to Gideon, "The LORD is with you, mighty warrior" (6:12). Mighty indeed! He was hiding.

Why Gideon? In a society where the oldest son was the most important and in a tribal system where the largest tribes provided the most soldiers, Gideon was the youngest ("least") son of an insignificant ("weakest") family in an unimportant tribe. Like Moses, he tried to beg off. Why would God choose an insignificant, frightened soldier-farmer?

How much faith did Gideon have? Not much. After his dramatic religious experience (6:11-24), he still demanded signs. Some people think that putting out a fleece was a sign of faith (6:36-40). In fact, it signaled a lack of faith. Recall that Jesus, when urged by Satan to jump from the pinnacle of the Temple, said, "Again it's written, *Don't test the Lord your God*" (Matthew 4:7).

Once again God chose the unlikely candidate.

The selection of three hundred men (Judges 7:4-8) always intrigues readers and scholars. Some interpret those three hundred who lapped water, putting their hands to their mouths, as tough mountain men with eyes flashing, always alert. But the biblical point is that God wanted a small group to show that the victory belonged not to humans but to God. Perhaps the divine-human alliance is the way God often works.

Samson

Samson was scarcely a judge. He did not call his people to corporate action. Rather, he cavorted his way through the enemy ranks, amusing his friends and dumbfounding his enemies. More like a Hercules than a prophet or military leader, Samson captures our imagination with his unusual strength, his romantic exploits, and his mischievous pranks.

Why did God give us the Samson story? Perhaps to help us understand devout parents who set apart their son to be a special person, a nazirite who neither cut his hair nor drank wine. Perhaps to help us laugh, since so much of the Bible is serious. Who can resist smiling at riddles about lions and honey? Perhaps to teach us, in sadness, how powerful persons can be brought low by "selling out" that holy vow that makes them special.

But Samson is probably in the Bible because he dramatically symbolizes the people of God—so human, so quick to act without

DISCIPLE FAST TRACK

thinking, so prone to folly. We are set apart to be a holy people, capable of great strength against formidable foes, yet weakened by sin, blinded by the enemy, but able through the power of God to experience forgiveness and rise from the ashes to strike a blow for freedom once again.

MARKS OF DISCIPLESHIP

God calls leaders to give people a sense of direction and purpose. When the leaders are godly, they give sound direction; when they are disobedient or ambivalent, they lead people astray.

What kind of people do you think God chooses as leaders?

What does it mean to place yourself under the authority of your spiritual leaders?

Describe a time God called you to be a leader.

NOTES

Mark of Discipleship
Disciples provide a sense of direction and purpose through godly, obedient leadership.

58

Some homes display a plaque that reads, "Christ is the head of this house." How is such a motto lived out in daily life?

Describe what would happen if in your country or your church or your household "each person did what they thought to be right" (Judges 21:25).

IF YOU WANT TO KNOW MORE

One of the most beautiful stories ever written is the Book of Ruth, a love story about David's great-grandmother during the time of the judges, but quite unlike the Book of Judges. Perhaps on your seventh day, you could simply read and enjoy the story of Ruth.

"If you will fear the LORD, worship him, obey him, and not rebel against the LORD's command, and if both you and the king who rules over you follow the LORD your God—all will be well. But if you don't obey the LORD and rebel against the LORD's command, then the LORD's power will go against you and your king to destroy you."
—1 Samuel 12:14-15

8 The People With a King

OUR HUMAN CONDITION

We demand leaders, hoping they will bring security and peace. We want our leaders to make decisions for us, to tell us what to do so we won't have to take responsibility for ourselves and our actions. But power tends to corrupt; and we discover our leaders, like us, have feet of clay.

ASSIGNMENT

This week we read fascinating narratives of explosive emotions and human and divine interactions. The characters are some of the most colorful in Scripture—people like Hannah, Eli, Samuel, Saul, Jonathan, David, Bathsheba, Absalom, Solomon, and the queen of Sheba. You must read rapidly to cover so much story material.

Pray daily before study:

"I will give thanks to you, my LORD,
    among all the peoples;
I will make music to you among
    the nations
 because your faithful love is as high
    as heaven;
 your faithfulness reaches the clouds.
 Exalt yourself, God, higher than heaven!
 Let your glory be over all the earth!"
                (Psalm 57:9-11).

Prayer concerns for the week:

Day 1 **Read 1 Samuel 1–3; 7:3-17** (Samuel).

Day 4 **Read 2 Samuel 7–8:1, 11-12** (God's covenant with David, David and Bathsheba).

Day 2 **Read 1 Samuel 8–10; 12** (Saul, Samuel's farewell address).

Day 5 **Read 1 Kings 1–2:12; 3; 4:20-34; 5–6:14; 7:1-12; 8; 11–12** (David's death, Solomon's prayer, building and dedicating the Temple, Solomon's apostasy).

Day 3 **Read 1 Samuel 14:47–19:24; 31** (Saul rejected, David anointed king, David and Goliath, David and Jonathan, death of Saul).

Day 6 **Read "The Bible Teaching" and the "Marks of Discipleship" and answer the questions.**

Day 7 **Rest, pray, and attend class.**

DISCIPLE FAST TRACK

THE BIBLE TEACHING

Did God's people want a king? Yes and no. Samuel was ambivalent. He actually anointed both Saul and David, yet he argued against the idea of kingship. First and Second Samuel, originally one book, have different threads of tradition. Some threads affirm kingdom; others declare kingdom a big mistake.

The Bible does not back away from ambivalence. Confusion clouds all human experience. The Bible records that confusion. On one hand, a king might bring cohesiveness and greater security. On the other hand, as Samuel stated (1 Samuel 8:10-18), a king could increase taxes, conscript an army, and restrict personal liberty. A faithful king might lead the people along a righteous path, but a disobedient king could lead them to tragic ends.

Even more important was the question of the people's relationship to God. The religious ideal of the people was to obey God and to live together in harmony. Leaders like Moses, Joshua, and Samuel had hoped that God would be King of the Israelites. Their security would rest in God.

But the people were like Adam and Eve—disobedient, afraid, vulnerable, and estranged. They were like Cain—hostile and jealous. They were like those who built the tower of Babel— proudly wanting to guarantee their own future. They went off in all directions: "In those days there was no king in Israel; each person did what they thought to be right" (Judges 21:25).

The people cried to Samuel, "Appoint us a king to judge us like all the other nations have" (1 Samuel 8:5). Samuel prayed, and God said, "They haven't rejected you [Samuel]. No, they've rejected me as king over them. . . . So comply with their request, but give them a clear warning, telling them how the king will rule over them" (8:7, 9).

The pressure for unity intensified with the coming of the Philistines. The loose union of Hebrew tribes had fought fairly well against Canaanites and neighboring groups such as the Amorites, the Moabites, and the Midianites. But around 1200 B.C. a powerful group called Philistines settled along the coastal plain. They used advanced technology, including iron weapons and chariots. Under strong leadership and living in five tightly coordinated city states (Ashkelon, Ashdod, Gath, Ekron, and Gaza), the Philistines raided practically at will. In their temples they worshiped many fertility gods—the god Dagon (chief god of the Philistine city states) in Ashdod and Gaza, the goddess Astarte in Ashkelon, and Baal-zebub in Ekron. Israel thus faced a unified and powerful enemy.

Samuel

The story begins with a childless couple, Elkanah and Hannah. Hannah prayed so fervently for a child that the priest presumed she was drunk. The Lord answered Hannah's prayers, and she gave birth to Samuel.

Identify the place of worship (1 Samuel 1:3) that was Israel's most important religious center until David took the capital to Jerusalem.

Samuel grew up to be God's man. He was the last of the great judges and the first of the great prophets. Like Moses, he was nursed on his mother's faith but raised by another. In this case Samuel was raised by Eli the priest, who, after failing with his own sons, Hophni and Phinehas, tried extra hard to instill dedication in the young boy entrusted to his care. Hannah gave her son the name *Samuel*, which probably meant "name of God," though Hannah explained its meaning as "I asked the LORD for him" (1 Samuel 1:20). Samuel became the prophet who was to anoint the first two kings of Israel.

Saul

Saul physically stood head and shoulders above other men (1 Samuel 9:2). He experienced religious ecstasy (19:18-24). He earned the respect and love of brave men, including David (2 Samuel 1:19-24).

Samuel anointed Saul to be king but gave him a continual stream of divine commands. There was no room for Saul to make a mistake. Samuel gave mixed support in 1 Samuel 12. Then in 1 Samuel 13, Samuel put Saul to the test at Gilgal. It seems to have been an unfair test, because Saul waited the agreed-upon seven days, yet Samuel did not come. With his army scattering, Saul went ahead and offered the sacrifices himself. Samuel then arrived and accused the king, "You have broken the commands the LORD your God gave you! . . . Now your rule won't last" (13:13-14). On one hand, Samuel seemed to speak clearly a divine word; on the other hand, he seemed to reveal an old man's unwillingness to yield power.

Saul spent his entire reign struggling to keep his authority intact. By sparing King Agag and the best sheep and cattle in the battle with Amalek, he disobeyed the divine command (1 Samuel 15). He became increasingly anxious about his throne, slipped into depression, and finally descended into paranoia.

Later, when David said, "Look how the mighty warriors have fallen" (2 Samuel 1:19; also see verses 19-27), he could have been referring to Saul's personality deterioration as well as to Saul's defeat and death in battle.

David

In April, Jerusalem bursts forth in beauty. Perfume is in the air on a spring evening. The love poem attributed by tradition to Solomon expresses this atmosphere romantically:

"Rise up, my dearest,
      my fairest, and go.
Here, the winter is past;
      the rains have come and gone.
Blossoms have appeared in the land;
      the season of singing has arrived,
      and the sound of the turtledove is heard in
            our land.
The green fruit is on the fig tree,
      and the grapevines in bloom are fragrant.
Rise up, my dearest,
      my fairest, and go" (Song of Solomon 2:10-13).

April is also a time for war, after the cold winter and the spring rains have ended (2 Samuel 11:1). The troops of Israel were in the field. But David, mighty warrior, commander-in-chief, had chosen not to go but to run the war from the comfort of the capital.

King David, now middle-aged, took a walk on his roof and saw in the courtyard below the strikingly beautiful wife of one of his elite soldiers, bathing in the late afternoon sun.

The rest of the story reads like the morning newspaper: an evening romance, an unwanted pregnancy, an anxious conversation, and a frantic search for a cover-up plan.

The cover-up seemed to have worked. Then, in one of the Bible's most dramatic encounters, David listened to the prophet Nathan tell a simple story of a grave injustice. The prophet pointed an accusing finger at the king and said, "You are that man!" (12:7).

David had so much to offer. A natural-born leader, an athlete, and a soldier, he also became a skilled politician who unified Israel.

David was God's man. His faith was strong, his loyalty to God was sure, and his personal ambition blended well with the needs of his nation.

But he sinned. He shattered the commandments of Moses as if he had broken the tablets into fragments:

You shall not covet Uriah's wife.
You shall not commit adultery with Bathsheba.
You shall not kill your faithful soldier-companion.
You shall not bear false witness to the nation.

In one act of passionate rebellion against God, David betrayed his divinely anointed leadership. Read again the fervent prayer of repentance (Psalm 51) that has been called David's prayer.

To say "I'm sorry" removes guilt but not consequences. The kingdom was shaken by family unfaithfulness. David was judged unworthy to build the Temple. The line to Solomon was marred.

Still, even in his sin and repentance, David was God's man, and Israel would always remember "the kingdom of David" as a golden era of unity and strength.

Solomon

Solomon was born rich. He was as crazy about wheels as any sixteen-year-old kid. He bought his chariots from Egypt, his horses from Arabia. His stables sported forty thousand stalls. Solomon maintained a jet-set image—swimming pools, summer homes, winter palaces. Even the queen of Sheba came to visit and gaze at the opulence of Solomon's court. Wives were a status symbol, and Solomon had seven hundred wives and three hundred concubines. Many of the marriages were political, personalizing foreign alliances. Solomon's family and court were so large that he needed one hundred sheep and thirty cattle a day to feed them.

During Solomon's reign, Israel buzzed with activity. Trade flourished. Construction boomed. The economy soared. Wise men from all over the kingdom established a school of wisdom. After Solomon built the Temple, he got the fever for government building programs. He pressed men into labor camps. He raised taxes (Samuel had warned that this would happen). King Solomon enlarged the army. He even developed a national navy. He stripped Lebanon of its trees so that cedar in Jerusalem became as common as sycamore.

Before the bubble burst, the splendor of Solomon's kingdom was the talk of the world. Later, Jesus even spoke of "Solomon in all of his splendor" (Matthew 6:29). But when the country crumbled, the fall was faster than the rise. Men were weary of conscription, tired of the huge bureaucracy, outraged by the arrogance in the capital. Solomon's majestic palace was twice as big as the Temple.

Solomon's big trouble, according to Scripture, was with God. He had prayed for wisdom (1 Kings 3:6-9), and God had granted it. Solomon was wise. But he forgot. He forgot that he stood in a line with Abraham and Joseph, Moses and Samuel, Saul and David. He forgot that he and his people were slaves whom God had delivered from Egypt. In his old age he worshiped the gods of his foreign wives, and the integrity of the covenant people was compromised. Solomon's sin was apostasy. He forgot who he was. He forgot who God is.

At Solomon's death the kingdom came crashing down. It broke into northern and southern kingdoms, its spiritual and political unity destroyed, and one day it would be trampled underfoot by the great armies of the world.

Moses had warned, "Don't forget the LORD your God. . . . When you eat, get full, build nice houses, and settle down, and when your herds and your flocks are growing large, your silver and gold are multiplying, and everything you have is thriving, . . . don't think to yourself, My own strength and abilities have produced all this prosperity for me" (Deuteronomy 8:11-17). Solomon forgot.

The kings of Israel reenacted the sins described in Genesis. Saul, like Adam and Eve, disobeyed, and the kingdom was taken from him.

David, like Cain who killed his brother Abel, passionately rebelled, and Uriah's blood cried out, "You are that man!" Solomon, like the builders of the tower of Babel, arrogantly tried to build a city and

NOTES

a name for himself. He was apostate, and the kingdom came tumbling down.

The fortunes of the people went from bad to worse. Rehoboam threatened to increase the already heavy burden his father Solomon had laid on the people. The northern tribes withdrew and made Jeroboam their king. Under his leadership apostasy reigned in the Northern Kingdom.

MARKS OF DISCIPLESHIP

The disciple keeps a proper perspective on human leadership, giving respect and support to godly leaders but true allegiance only to God.

Why do people put such high hopes in their leaders?

What kinds of actions and attitudes of leaders do you think God blesses? What kinds of actions and attitudes demonstrate faithfulness to God's will?

List some ways you can give support and encouragement to public and church leaders right now, helping them avoid tragedy.

Mark of Discipleship
Disciples maintain a perspective on leadership that supports and respects godly leaders but give true allegiance only to God.

IF YOU WANT TO KNOW MORE

The biblical tradition puts considerable emphasis on Solomon's construction and dedication of the Temple (1 Kings 6–8). Bible dictionaries and handbooks often have drawings of what the Temple and its furnishings might have looked like. Prepare a report for the group using the biblical text and visuals you can locate.

NOTES

"The LORD said to me, 'Amos, what do you see?'
'A plumb line,' I said. Then the LORD said, 'See,
I am setting a plumb line in the middle of my people
Israel. I will never again forgive them.'" —Amos 7:8

9 God Warns the People

OUR HUMAN CONDITION

Generally we do not heed warnings until too late.
We hate to be told we are doing wrong. We don't
really believe that severe punishment will come to
us. Leave us alone. We are getting along fine. We
will call you when we need you.

ASSIGNMENT

The prophets delivered God's word to the
people. They often spoke the word of warning.
Different prophets, different times, different sins,
yet always the same theme: Because of your
disobedience and unfaithfulness to your covenant
God, punishment is coming to Israel.

As you read, keep three time periods in mind:
• Elijah and Elisha (ninth century B.C.)
• Amos and Isaiah 1–39 (eighth century B.C.)
• Jeremiah (seventh to sixth centuries B.C.)

Pray daily before study:

"Won't you bring us back to life again
  so that your people can rejoice in you?
Show us your faithful love, LORD!
  Give us your salvation!" (Psalm 85:6-7).

Prayer concerns for the week:

Day 1 **Read 1 Kings 16:29–19:18** (Elijah and Ahab).

Day 2 **Read 1 Kings 21–22** (Ahab, Naboth's vineyard).

Day 3 **Read Amos 2:6–4:13** (repeated warnings).

Day 4 **Read Amos 5; 7:1-9; 9** (lament and visions of Amos, a plumb line in Samaria).

Day 5 **Read Isaiah 3–6** (rebellious Judah, Isaiah's call).

Day 6 **Read "The Bible Teaching" and the "Marks of Discipleship" and answer the questions.**

Day 7 **Rest, pray, and attend class.**

THE BIBLE TEACHING

The prophets understood the tension that existed between Israel's religion and the pagan practices of neighboring peoples. Also, the prophets clearly discerned the difference between a righteous, faithful people and a popular, comfortable religiosity.

In their finest moments, the prophets called the people of God to remember their deep roots:

> "What the LORD requires from you:
>   to do justice, embrace faithful love, and
>   walk humbly with your God" (Micah 6:8).

The Hebrew word for "prophet" is *nabi*, a common noun used over three hundred times in the Old Testament. It means "one who is called" or "one who announces." Early prophets were "seers," or "visionaries," who received their messages from God through visions or dreams and gave signs, warnings, and predictions. In the early period, ecstatic religious experience characterized groups or schools of prophets. (See 1 Samuel 10:10-12.) Later, another dimension of prophecy developed. Prophets saw God interacting with history.

The prophet clearly believes that God enters decisively into human history. The prophet "sees," "hears," or "understands" what God is doing or is going to do and, often at great personal peril, announces that reality to the people.

Fire burns in their bones (Jeremiah 20:9) to tell the message the way God has told it to them. They may be speaking to kings, as Nathan spoke to David about Uriah (2 Samuel 12) and as Elijah spoke to Ahab about Naboth's vineyard (1 Kings 21), or to people and nations as Amos spoke to the Northern Kingdom. But they all have a sense of being called to announce God's words and God's actions.

Before the time of the kings of Israel, some people who were political and military leaders were termed prophets. Miriam and Deborah (Exodus 15:20-21; Judges 4:4) were called prophets because they played eloquent roles in celebrating God's relationship with the people of Israel. Moses was called a prophet, not only because he knew God "face to face" but because he reported what God told him. "I'll raise up a prophet for them from among their fellow Israelites—one just like you. I'll put my words in his mouth, and he will tell them everything I command him" (Deuteronomy 18:18).

Paganism

The prophets were opposed to two things—paganism and injustice. Paganism meant not putting God first in their lives. It meant flirting with the gods of other tribes and nations, forgetting their unique covenant community. If they ate unclean foods, neglected the sabbath, intermarried with foreign peoples, worshiped on high hills (a practice of Baal worship), then they were "acting like a prostitute" (Jeremiah 2:20). If Israel was to be God's chosen people, they must be a peculiar people. If Israel was to be a "light to the nations" (Isaiah 42:6), they must be an obedient people.

King Ahab (869–850 B.C.) ruled the Northern Kingdom, called Israel. The prophet Elijah was furious because Ahab married Jezebel, a foreign princess, and permitted her to establish Baal worship as an acceptable practice in Israel (1 Kings 16:29-33).

Notice that King Ahab accused Elijah of being a troublemaker. People always accuse prophets of being troublemakers because they point out evil. "Elijah answered, 'I haven't troubled Israel; you and your father's house have! You did as much when you deserted the LORD's commands and followed the Baals' " (1 Kings 18:18).

Then came the great contest between Elijah and the prophets of Baal on Mount Carmel. The contest was a spiritual crisis, a national watershed. Was Israel to be God's people or not? Everything was at stake, as far as Elijah was concerned. The prophets of Baal were killed, and Queen Jezebel vowed revenge.

Jezebel threatened to kill the prophet. Why didn't King Ahab make the threat? Because the people of Israel had an amazing willingness to allow the word of the prophet in their midst. Can you imagine a king in another culture permitting chastisement like Nathan gave David over Uriah or like Elijah gave Ahab over Naboth's vineyard?

Elijah warned Israel about paganism.

Injustice

The second concern of the prophets was injustice. When Israel and Judah did not put God first in their lives, they began to put themselves first. (We do the same.) As a result, they lacked consideration for neighbor and compassion for the weak. The prophets, sensing destruction was coming, first from Assyria and then from Babylon, announced these disasters as punishment. The people of Israel, they warned, would be destroyed and exiled because of their refusal to take seriously their covenant responsibility for compassion and justice.

Religious responsibilities, political responsibilities, and economic responsibilities—all of life was included in the divine perspective. God's vision was a new social community in which everyone would be an integral part. A radically free God was trying to form a radically just and caring people! God wanted the covenant people to model justice to the world.

"There won't be any poor persons among you . . . only if you carefully obey the LORD your God's voice. . . . You must open your hand generously to your fellow Israelites, to the needy among you, and to the poor who live with you in your land" (Deuteronomy 15:4-5, 11).

But Israel failed. Self-interest prevailed. Love of God declined; so did love of neighbor. Look in Amos for descriptions of social wickedness. Remember that transgression or sinning again and again is not just failing or forgetting. It is aggressive rebellion, active revolt against the established authority of almighty God.

Write in your own words the sins against neighbor described in Amos 2:6-8 and 4:1-3.

Do the same with Amos 5:10-13 and 6:4-7. Notice that insensitivity and aloofness in the face of human suffering are considered covenant betrayals.

In Amos's vision, the Lord drops a plumb line in the midst of Israel (7:8). Israel does not line up with God's will. Look at the greed, the materialistic fever in 8:4-6. Describe in your own words this burning desire for money. How would you compare it to our attitudes toward economic matters? (Be careful now: Jobs are important; money is necessary; yet frenzy and greed violate God's law.)

Of special importance, Amos, like other prophets, condemned religious ceremony when carried on in indifference to social justice. He expressed this with intense feeling:

"I hate, I reject your festivals" (5:21) (prescribed in Leviticus).
"Take away the noise of your songs" (5:23) (psalms and worship services).
"But let justice roll down like waters,
    and righteousness like an ever-flowing
        stream" (5:24).

The warnings are proclaimed. They do not come from human beings. They come from God with a roar through the "one who announces": through Amos, a shepherd from the little village of Tekoa in Judah (Amos 1:1); through Jeremiah, a boy (Jeremiah 1:4-9); through Isaiah, a sophisticated adviser in the king's court (Isaiah 6:1-8).

They preached, sometimes in dramatic fashion. Isaiah walked naked through the streets as a warning against Judah's joining Egypt against Assyria (Isaiah 20). They sometimes gave their children symbolic names (Isaiah 8:1-4). Hosea named a child "Not my people" to show the nation's apostasy (Hosea 1:4-9). Sometimes they used symbolic actions. Jeremiah broke a clay jug near a gate to Jerusalem to symbolize the coming destruction (Jeremiah 19). But the nation would not listen.

Some of the hardest words were given to Isaiah:

" 'Go and say to this people:
"Listen intently, but don't understand;
    look carefully, but don't comprehend.' . . .
I said, 'How long, Lord?'
And God said, 'Until cities lie ruined with no one living in them, until there are houses without people and the land is left devastated.' The LORD will send the people far away" (Isaiah 6:9, 11-12).

The people were warned about injustice, but they would not listen.

MARKS OF DISCIPLESHIP

Prophets still warn us, but in different ways.
Doctors predict our health risks if we do not change our habits.
Evangelists show a heavenly path and a hellish path and plead for decision.
Social prophets point to racial injustice and are called troublemakers, point to environmental pollutants and are called anti-business, condemn abuse of power and are regarded as unpatriotic.

Mark of Discipleship
Disciples recognize and listen to prophetic voices raised about community, nation, and world and at times become the prophetic voice.

Is someone right now saying something prophetic in the biblical sense for you, for your community, for your nation, or for your world? How are you listening to the warning?

Describe a time you felt God's Spirit placing in your mouth a holy warning that you felt called upon to give to others.

IF YOU WANT TO KNOW MORE

We did not read about the prophet Hosea. Hosea's wife Gomer left him for other men, and Hosea bought her back as God will buy back an unfaithful people. If you have time, read Hosea's dramatic social witness.

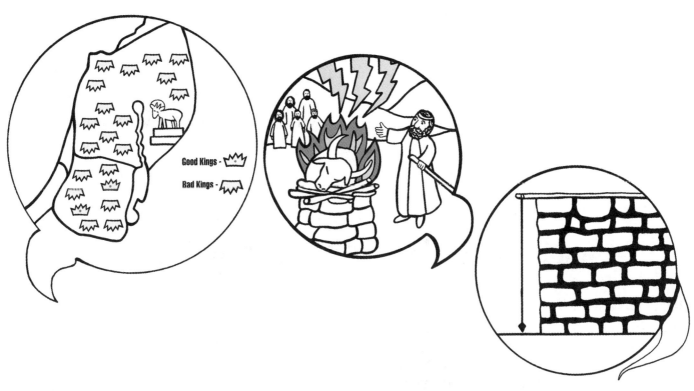

WARNING

"Haven't you brought this on yourself
by abandoning the LORD your God,
who has directed your paths?"
—Jeremiah 2:17

10 God Punishes the People

OUR HUMAN CONDITION

We think we can sidestep the consequences of our sins, but we cannot. We deceive ourselves. We think religious practices will save us. We think wealth or prestige will protect us. But we are held accountable. Then we respond to punishment by denying; blaming others; and displaying anger, depression, and despair. Often we refuse comfort and even deny new possibilities. We think all is lost.

ASSIGNMENT

In the Scriptures there are consequences to sin, yet God is present to comfort in the midst of them. Israel and Judah are on a judgment course, and no words or actions will change it. But pay attention to the presence and action of God. Watch as God both judges and holds out the offer and hope of redemption. Absorb the many words of comfort and hope spoken while Israel experiences the consequences.

Pray daily before study:

"Please, for the sake of your good
name, LORD, forgive my sins,
which are many!" (Psalm 25:11).

Prayer concerns for the week:

Day 1 **Read 2 Kings 17** (fall of the Northern Kingdom); **2 Kings 18–20** (King Hezekiah of the Southern Kingdom).

Day 2 **Read 2 Kings 22:1-2; 23** (King Josiah's reforms in the Southern Kingdom); **2 Kings 25** (fall of the Southern Kingdom).

Day 3 **Read Jeremiah 8** (warnings to the Southern Kingdom before the fall); **Jeremiah 37–39** (Jeremiah imprisoned); **Isaiah 28:16-26** (warnings to Jerusalem); **Lamentations 1** (Jeremiah's sorrow over Jerusalem).

Day 4 **Read Isaiah 40; 42:1-9; 43:1-13** (words of comfort in exile); **44:21-23** (Israel the chosen), **49** (God's help); **55** (God's offer of mercy).

Day 5 **Read Ezekiel 1–3:15** (Ezekiel's call); **Ezekiel 37** (vision of valley of dry bones); **Jeremiah 31–32** (the new covenant).

Day 6 **Read "The Bible Teaching" and the "Marks of Discipleship" and answer the questions or provide responses.**

Day 7 **Rest, pray, and attend class.**

THE BIBLE TEACHING

Consequences

The destruction actually came to the Northern Kingdom (Israel, capital city Samaria) by the Assyrians in 722/721 B.C. and to the Southern Kingdom (Judah, capital city Jerusalem) in 587/586 B.C. by the Babylonians.

Moses' exhortation to obedience in Deuteronomy now rings true: "Once you have had children and grandchildren and have grown old on the land, if you ruin things by making an idol, in any form whatsoever, and do what is evil in the eyes of the LORD your God and anger him, I call heaven and earth as my witnesses against you today: You will definitely disappear—and quickly—from the land that you are crossing over the Jordan River to possess. You won't extend your time there but will instead be totally destroyed. The LORD will scatter you among the nations" (Deuteronomy 4:25-27).

Much interpretation and reinterpretation is interwoven. As you read Second Kings, you read first of the destruction of the Northern Kingdom and then of the destruction of the Southern Kingdom, particularly the destruction of the Temple and the fall of Jerusalem.

The prophets made two points when interpreting these events:

First, the people of God brought it on themselves. They had been warned by a "slow to anger" God. They could not blame anybody else, nor could they blame foreign gods more powerful than their own. The one true God of the universe called them into accountability.

Near the end, the people made several "last-ditch" efforts to no avail. The sickness was too deep:

> "Everyone's head throbs,
>   and everyone's heart fails.
> From head to toe, none are well" (Isaiah 1:5-6).

Second, the search for salvation took the form of a desperate desire for military alliances with other nations.

With armies coming down from the north, the leaders decided to put their trust in the Egyptians. Prophets like Isaiah warned the leaders. Egypt was a broken reed, dangerous to lean upon. They should trust God alone and not alliances with foreigners. They had more chance of survival as an independent nation with integrity than as a vacillating ally of the enemy of Assyria and Babylon.

The Tears of the Prophets for Israel and Judah

Do not think the prophets were eager to announce the calamity. The message they gave broke their hearts. They loved the Lord, the covenant, the Temple, the people, and their homeland.

> "No healing,
>   only grief;
>   my heart is broken. . . .

> Because my people are crushed
>   I am crushed;
>   darkness and despair overwhelm me"
>   (Jeremiah 8:18, 21).

Nothing, not even the tears of the prophets, could stop the dire consequences of apostasy and rebellion, infidelity and social injustice. Institutions would topple. Kings and princes would be led away in chains. The brightest and best would be tied to chariots and led like animals into captivity. The government, established by God, would go down in ruins. The land of promise, flowing with "milk and honey," would be burned and made desolate. The economy would be destroyed. The Temple, built by Solomon on the site chosen by David, would be razed. All would be lost.

The Takeover of the Northern Kingdom (Israel)

Sure enough, in the eighth century B.C., following the preaching and prophesying of Amos, Hosea, Micah, and Isaiah, the Assyrians marched down the coastline. Based in their capital, Nineveh, the Assyrians ambitiously set out to rule the world. By 722/721 B.C., when the Northern Kingdom (Israel) fell to Assyria, pure political independence by small neighboring states was impossible.

In Israel, as predicted, many leading citizens and skilled people were taken captive to various regions of the Assyrian Empire. In exchange, several thousand people from throughout the empire were transported into Israel. That political process was designed to break down national pride and help unify the Assyrian kingdom. In time the conquered peoples brought into Israel intermarried with the remaining Israelites, and their descendants became the people known as the Samaritans.

The Takeover of the Southern Kingdom (Judah)

The little Southern Kingdom (Judah), barely surviving by paying duty, now had a brief respite. With lessening political pressure from outside, Judah's King Josiah (640–609 B.C.) instituted significant reform. Josiah was so moved on hearing the words of the newly discovered book of the Law (the earliest form of Deuteronomy) that he restored purity in worship, maintained integrity in government, and established social legislation (2 Kings 22–23). Josiah abolished cult prostitution and Assyrian and Babylonian practices of star and animal worship. He reestablished Passover and rearticulated the law of Moses.

But the time of reform was short-lived. The Babylonians moved into the political vacuum on the outside, and with Josiah's death in 609 B.C., the internal spirit in Judah dissipated. Judah fell back into old ways. Josiah's efforts weren't enough. Repentance is more than reform in worship. Repentance means reorienting your lifestyle, placing the Lord first in all your ways (Deuteronomy 4:25-40).

The Babylonians ravaged Jerusalem, razed the Temple, killed King Zedekiah's sons right before his eyes, then gouged out his

DISCIPLE FAST TRACK

eyes and led him and thousands of others into Babylonian captivity (2 Kings 25:6-7; Jeremiah 39:6-9).

Hope

Yet . . .

The people will be like a tree, cut down. Then the stump will be burned, but "its stump is a holy seed" (Isaiah 6:13).

God's purpose is not to destroy but to chastise, not to annihilate but to purify and redeem. Do not read the prophets as proclaiming unqualified, unrelieved doom. Even when the punishment is fulfilled, there is a glimmer of hope. For God is not the same as the Temple. Though the Temple is destroyed, God is not dead. Though the Promised Land is ravaged, the God of promise lives and rules. Though most of the people are dispersed or dead, a remnant will survive.

But most of us cannot see that ray of hope when our world caves in around us. We are just like the lamenting exiles, thinking revenge rather than repentance.

> "Alongside Babylon's streams,
>   there we sat down,
>   crying because we remembered Zion. . . .
> But how could we possibly sing
>   the LORD's song on foreign soil? . . .
> Daughter Babylon, you destroyer, . . .
>   A blessing on the one who seizes your children
>   and smashes them against the rock!"
>   (Psalm 137:1, 4, 8-9).

There is no turning back. The judgment of God has come.

Comfort

From the beginning, God's punishment was never total destruction. God's grace works even amid retribution. Remember, God clothed Adam and Eve even as God drove them from the garden of innocence. Cain was marked for protection, Noah and his family were spared from the Flood, and the Lord saved Lot and his family from Sodom and Gomorrah.

Isaiah of Jerusalem, whose work is found in Isaiah 1–39, when he was called to be a prophet (Isaiah 6:1-8), knew the people would not listen. God would make the land desolate in spite of Isaiah's pleas for repentance. Yet God would still let Israel live. Though the tree be cut down, "its stump is a holy seed" (6:13). There would be a remnant.

Jeremiah, when the armies of Babylon were only a few miles from Jerusalem and real estate prices had totally collapsed, bought a field and had the title registered to show his faith in the future (Jeremiah 32:6-15).

Ezekiel, while still in exile, was swept up in a vision and saw in a valley of dry bones a hope that Israel would be a living people again (Ezekiel 37).

Kings and Prophets (selected) of the Northern Kingdom—Israel (approximate dates B.C.)

Kings	Prophets
Jeroboam I (922–901)	Ahijah
Omri (876–869)	Jehu
Ahab (869–850)	Elijah
Ahaziah (850–849)	Elijah
Jehoram/Joram (849–842)	Elisha
Jehu (842–815)	Elisha
Jehoash/Joash (801–786)	Elisha
Jeroboam II (786–746)	Hosea
	Amos
Pekahiah (738–737)	Micah
Pekah (737–732)	Micah
Hoshea (732–721)	Micah
	Hosea
Fall of Samaria to Assyria (722/721)	

Kings and Prophets (selected) of the Southern Kingdom—Judah (approximate dates B.C.)

Kings	Prophets
Rehoboam (922–915)	Shemaiah
Jehoshaphat (873–849)	Jehu
Jehoram/Joram (849–842)	Elijah
Ahaziah (842 only)	Jehu
Joash/Jehoash (837–800)	Jehoiada
	Joel
	Zechariah
Amaziah (800–783)	Unnamed
Uzziah (783–742)	Zechariah
	Amos
	Isaiah
	Hosea
Jotham (742–735)	Isaiah
	Micah
	Hosea
Ahaz (735–715)	Isaiah
	Micah
Hezekiah (715–687)	Nahum
	Isaiah
	Micah
	Hosea
Manasseh (687–642)	Unnamed
Josiah (640–609)	Huldah
	Zephaniah
	Jeremiah
Jehoiakim (609–597)	Jeremiah
Zedekiah (597–587)	Jeremiah
Fall of Jerusalem to Babylon (587/586)	

CONSEQUENCES

In Israel's dark hour, God spoke a word of consolation:

> "Comfort, O comfort my people. . . .
> Speak compassionately to Jerusalem"
> (Isaiah 40:1-2).

Why? Because "her penalty has been paid"; that is, her exile, her punishment, is ended. Recall that here the prophet was writing near the end of the Exile.

The destruction had been severe, very severe; and everyone had suffered, even the innocent. The punishment had been double measure (40:2). Now was the time for tenderness. "He will gather lambs in his arms" (40:11).

The comfort comes from God just as the punishment came from God. Idols are a laughing matter. We still have to deal with almighty God.

God reaffirms the covenant with the servant Israel. Justice has been reestablished (42:1-4). The price has been paid. In a beautiful image reminiscent of Moses passing through the sea and Joshua crossing the Jordan, God says,

> "Don't fear, for I have redeemed you;
>   I have called you by name; you are mine.
> When you pass through the waters, I will be
>   with you;
>   when through the rivers, they won't sweep
>   over you" (43:1-2).

When the Temple lay in ruins and the people killed or in exile, surely countless Judeans cried out with the psalmist,

> "My God! My God,
>   why have you left me all alone?" (Psalm 22:1).

But God claims eternal kinship.

> "Can a woman forget her nursing child,
>   fail to pity the child of her womb?
>   Even these may forget,
>   but I won't forget you.
> Look, on my palms I've inscribed you"
> (Isaiah 49:15-16).

What a foretaste of the nails in the hands of Christ!

A Light to the Nations

King Cyrus of Persia gave permission for the people to return to Jerusalem and rebuild the Temple. You would think it enough for Israel to be going home rejoicing. But no, God has more for the servant Israel. They are not finished with their mission. Were they not called in Abraham and Sarah to be blessed in order to be a blessing (Genesis 12:2-3)? God wants them to take their witness, their sense of justice, their understanding of God, and now their chastisement and disciplined experience to use it to witness to the whole world.

Treating Israel as if the nation were a single individual—a servant—God says it is too easy just to return home.

> "He said: It is not enough, since you are my servant,
> to raise up the tribes of Jacob
> and to bring back the survivors of Israel.
> Hence, I will also appoint you as light to the nations
> so that my salvation may reach to the end of the earth"
> (Isaiah 49:6).

But how will that be done? In a most perplexing way: by being a servant, a suffering servant. Kings will be speechless to see so unattractive, so marred a servant (52:14-15). Israel's remnant suffered vicariously for the sins of the whole world. "He carried the sin of many" (53:12). No wonder this great suffering servant passage astonished Israel. No wonder the Gospel writers and early church saw it as one of the great prophetic messages about Jesus' crucifixion.

God has a purpose in all of this, Isaiah argues. Welcome, thirsty exiles; come and drink.

God Is Everywhere

We cannot understand God's punishment and restoration. It is a great mystery. But Ezekiel did learn something important about the God of Israel in one of his holy visions. One day Ezekiel was sitting beside the "river" Chebar in Babylon. He had been one of those strong, intelligent young men roped to the chariots of Nebuchadnezzar in the first exile group (597 B.C.) before the final fall of Jerusalem. He was lonely for God and homesick. Did not the God of Abraham reside in Jerusalem? Did not the God of Moses dwell in the ark of the covenant in the Temple?

Each creature went straight forward. Wherever the Spirit would go, they went, without turning as they went. "Aha," thought Ezekiel. "No turning, no deviation from God's purpose. The Lord will carry out whatever the Lord wills!"

"As I looked at the creatures, suddenly there was a wheel on the earth corresponding to all four faces of the creatures. . . . When they moved in any of the four directions, they moved without swerving. . . . When the creatures moved, the wheels moved next to them" (1:15-19).

"I understand!" cried Ezekiel. Those chariot wheels, turning, turning, rolling away from Jerusalem, were not rolling away from God! God was in the wheels. God moved with the movement. The God of the universe was everywhere. Now the people of Israel could sing the Lord's song in a foreign land, in any land (Psalm 137:4)!

The impact of this understanding on Judaism was tremendous. Jews began to gather beside the "river" Chebar and beside the rivers in many other cities to sing the songs of Zion. They studied the law of Moses and debated and discussed it. They tried to keep certain Sabbath and dietary laws. They prayed together.

From these gatherings the synagogue was born. Far from the Temple, dispersed throughout the ancient world, the people of Israel found strength, peace, and solace in their ancient tradition, which they preserved for the day when the Temple would be restored and the sweet savor of their prayers would ascend to God along with the smoke of their sacrificial offerings. Even in exile, even in punishment, even in Babylon, God was with them.

From Ezekiel's vision, we comprehend a dynamic spiritual truth: God is with us no matter how far we travel geographically, no matter how far we go away from God spiritually, no matter how severe the tragedy, no matter how salty the tears.

As the psalmist declared,

> "Where could I go to get away from your
>   spirit?
> Where would I go to escape your presence?"
>   (Psalm 139:7).

MARKS OF DISCIPLESHIP

The disciple accepts the comfort of God and looks for new beginnings, fresh possibilities, new options. In suffering we choose between despair or creative service.

Write about a time when you felt you were disciplined and then comforted by God. Describe your feelings during the experience. Did you come through it with a feeling of being wounded? cleansed? comforted? Did it bring good to you? to others? You may or may not want to discuss this material with others.

Mark of Discipleship
Disciples accept the consequences of their sin, seek forgiveness, and look for healing and new opportunities for faithfulness. Disciples choose to serve rather than to despair when suffering the consequences of sin.

DISCIPLE FAST TRACK

Something human in us all makes us believe we never will be punished. We won't get caught. We'll be let off easy. We'll be given another chance.

Sometimes that is true. List some times when you were not held strictly accountable, when you were given a second chance.

But second chances run out, even for the disciple. The disciple accepts the consequences, asks for forgiveness, and looks for healing and new opportunities for faithfulness.

List some times when you were held strictly accountable and received the consequences of your actions.

IF YOU WANT TO KNOW MORE

The study of the word *comfort* is extremely interesting. Using a concordance, look up places where the word appears in the Bible. Use a dictionary and a Bible dictionary to study its meanings.

Assyrian Empire

Beth-Eden

Assyria

Israel and Judah

"Turn your ear toward wisdom, / and stretch your mind toward understanding. / Call out for insight, / and cry aloud for understanding. / Seek it like silver; / search for it like hidden treasure. / Then you will understand the fear of the LORD, / and discover the knowledge of God. / The LORD gives wisdom; / from his mouth come knowledge and understanding."
—Proverbs 2:2-6

11 God Responds to the People

OUR HUMAN CONDITION

We have questions about God and life. We hide parts of ourselves—certain feelings and thoughts—from God, ourselves, and others. We want to be healthy and happy, but on our own terms. Often we are not willing to pay the price that right living requires. Life isn't fair. Sometimes the wicked prosper and the good are cut down. Suffering bewilders us. Why did this happen? We need answers from God.

Pray daily before study:

"LORD, you have examined me.
  You know me.
You know when I sit down and when
    I stand up.
  Even from far away, you comprehend
    my plans.
You study my traveling and resting.
  You are thoroughly familiar with all
    my ways" (Psalm 139:1-3).

Prayer concerns for the week:

ASSIGNMENT

In this session we read great passages of wisdom literature from Psalms, Proverbs, and Job. We also continue to follow the story of the Hebrew people through Ezra and Nehemiah as they return to Jerusalem.

The Psalms mirror human emotions. They are songs, chants, prayers, liturgies, and responses meant to be used in corporate worship.

In Proverbs you will be looking for qualities that make for a just and peaceful world.

Job will grapple with the difficult questions of "why do bad things happen to faithful people?" As you read, consider the wisdom in these Scripture passages that are thousands of years old.

Day 1 **Read and complete "The Bible Teaching" under Day 1—Psalms on pages 87–89.**

Day 2 **Read and complete "The Bible Teaching" under Day 2—Psalms on pages 89–90.**

Day 3 **Read Proverbs 1. Read and complete "The Bible Teaching" under Day 3—Proverbs on pages 90–91.**

Day 4 Read Ezra 1; 3; 4:1-5; 7:8-10 (story of the return of the exiles to Jerusalem and the rebuilding of the Temple). **Read Nehemiah 1; 2; 4:15-23; 8:1–9:3; 10:28-39** (Reading of the Law and renewing the Covenant). **Read and complete "The Bible Teaching" under Day 4—Ezra and Nehemiah on pages 91–92.**

Day 5 Read "The Bible Teaching" under Day 5—Job, including the marginal note about Satan, on page 92. Then read "The Job Drama" on pages 92–99. It is a condensed version of the entire Book of Job.

Day 6 Read Job 38; 42:1-6 (Job and God). **Read and respond to the "Marks of Discipleship" on page 99.**

Day 7 Rest, pray, and attend class.

THE BIBLE TEACHING
Day 1—Psalms

Jews and Christians of all persuasions and all ages claim the Psalms or Psalter. People revel in the Psalms for various reasons and approach them from different perspectives. The form and arrangement of the Psalms reflect classical Judaism. Psalm 1 extols the virtue of meditating on the Law (Torah), and Psalm 2 refers to God's anointed, literally "Messiah." Thus two cardinal beliefs of the Jewish people are quickly established: revelation of God's will in Torah and the concept of Messiah, the Anointed One to carry out God's purposes.

The Psalter is divided into five "books" to pattern after the five books of the Pentateuch (Torah). The Psalter was coming into being from the beginning of the people of Israel. Some psalms were written before the Exile, some during the Exile, and some after the Exile. The present form of the Psalms comes from the time of the second Temple in what is called the postexilic period.

The Psalter may also be called the prayer book of the synagogue. As the synagogues sprang up where Jews were dispersed all over the known world, the prayers helped Jews keep their faith and tradition alive.

The early Christians took the whole of the Hebrew Scriptures as their own, but the Psalms were especially precious. Jesus quoted most often from three sources: Deuteronomy (Moses and the Law), Isaiah, and the Psalms. The New Testament writers quoted most frequently from Psalms and Isaiah.

The earliest Christian disciples met in synagogues, singing psalms. They sang them in prison, feeling at one with the community of faith: "Around midnight Paul and Silas were praying and singing hymns to God, and the other prisoners were listening to them" (Acts 16:25). The writer of Ephesians encouraged believers to "be filled with the Spirit in the following ways: speak to each other with psalms, hymns, and spiritual songs; sing and make music to the Lord in your hearts" (Ephesians 5:18-19).

Today our study hopes not to teach you about the Psalms as much as to guide you into the Psalms. If you can let them help you express your inexpressible thoughts and feelings, they will become your prayers. Athanasius, a Christian leader in the fourth century A.D., said that most Scripture speaks to us but the Psalms speak for us. They are "songs of the heart," mirroring the totality of our human experiences.

The songs are corporate in nature, even when they are expressed in lonely agony. Always the one in prayer or song is aware of the historic covenant community, the faithful worshiping fellowship, and the encompassing arms of the Almighty. We learn to praise God, not just in times when we experience God's presence, but also in times when we feel God is absent. We sing while undergoing the severest of trials, when separated from the visible support of the Christian fellowship, but we are never alone.

Salvation History

Read Psalm 136. It recalls the salvation history of the Jews. Notice the corporate experience, the plural language, the sense of unity in Israel. Feel the beat from the powerful response, "God's faithful love lasts forever." Are we afraid, troubled, anxious, oppressed? Remember, "God's faithful love lasts forever." When are times that reading Psalm 136 would be helpful to you?

Lament

Read carefully Psalm 90. What feelings come to you?

In our society we try to disguise or even deny death; but when we declare this psalm beside the grave, we are open to our humanity. How does Psalm 90 help us face death more appropriately?

Penitence

Psalm 38 is an individual lament, a cry of distress, of regret, of penitence. Consider the many moods. Sickness seems coupled with sin. Describe your own memories of pain, loneliness, or guilt as you read these verses.

Day 2—Psalms

Thanksgiving

Psalm 65 expresses thankfulness as a community of faith. For what are the people thanking God?

For what might your congregation thank God?

Praise

Psalm 100 is pure praise. How do you want to praise God today?

Wisdom

Psalm 73 is a meditative "wisdom" psalm. In verses 2-3, how do you feel when the wicked prosper?

In verses 16-18, what did the psalmist come to understand?

Do you agree with the psalmist's understanding?

In verses 25-26, finally, what really matters?

Day 3—Proverbs

Proverbs teaches that the ways of God are good for us, and following them leads to a healthy, harmonious life. Evil ways cause great unhappiness, often resulting in sickness, poverty, broken relationships, injury, incapacity, and early death. Because we live in families and in community, individual sins and wickedness are often compounded into social catastrophe and institutionalized corruption. Also, sin weaves its way through the generations, causing the sins of the parents to be visited upon the children into the third and fourth generations (Exodus 20:5).

Proverbs concentrates on God's order repeated in human experience. How can we try to walk the godly path? The Bible gives us guidelines.

Consider integrity. As you read the following proverbs, notice what they say about:
- truthtelling (Proverbs 12:17; 12:22).
- honest measurement (Proverbs 11:1; 20:23).
- stealing (Proverbs 1:19).

How do these proverbs help us with right living?

Consider concern for the poor. As you read the following proverbs, notice what they say about:
- generosity (Proverbs11:25; 22:9; 25:21).
- hospitality to strangers (Proverbs 31:20).
- care for widows and orphans (Proverbs 15:25; 23:10).

Consider care for one's own family. As you read the following proverbs, notice what they say about:
- concern for teaching children (Proverbs1:8-9; 4:1-7).
- discipline of children (Proverbs 29:17).
- respect for elders and for spouse (Proverbs 16:31; 20:29).

Consider faithfulness to God. As you read the following proverbs, notice what they say about:

- faithfulness (Proverbs 3:1-6).
- prayers of the righteous (Proverbs 15:8; 15:29).
- first fruits as gifts (Proverbs 3:9-10).

Consider food and drink. Exercise in those hard, agricultural times was practically assured; yet the rich were sometimes chastised for obesity. As you read the following proverbs, notice what they say about:
- gluttony (Proverbs 23:2-3, 20-21).
- alcoholic drink (Proverbs 20:1; 21:17).

Day 4—Ezra and Nehemiah

Ezra and Nehemiah describe groups of exiles who returned to Jerusalem from Babylon. The idea that right living would bring divine approval became an obsession among some religious people. The Jews had experienced the ravages of war, captivity, and exile and were going home to begin again. As some of the Jewish leaders returned to Jerusalem, they wanted to avoid the sins of the past. They wanted to obey perfectly. They believed:
- that God would punish sin and reward righteousness;
- that keeping the Law offered great reward;
- that the covenant people must be pure, not intermarrying with foreign people who worshiped other gods and ate unclean foods;
- that the Temple and the holy offerings were a major part of faithfulness;
- that Sabbath laws were essential to righteousness;
- that everything they did must be built on reestablishment of the laws of the Torah;
- that sickness came from sin and that prosperity and health came from living in justice and righteousness.

God is just. Right living has great rewards. But as we will see in tomorrow's reading, this is not always the case. Sometimes sickness is not caused by sin. Sometimes the good are cut down. Sometimes the wicked prosper. Job raises these issues. So does Jesus later. But among the Jews a theology emerged that focused on the Temple, the Temple sacrifices, personal piety, the keeping of the Torah with great care, the separation of Jews (particularly in Jerusalem) from non-Jews, and the observance of holy days—the theology that religious people could live a pure and prosperous life.

Therefore Zerubbabel, governor of Judah and descendant of David, encouraged by the prophets Haggai and Zechariah, rebuilt the Temple. (This was the second Temple, as Solomon's Temple had been destroyed.) It was completed between 520 and 515 B.C.

Two expressions of Judaism developed—the Temple, emphasizing sacrifice, and the synagogue, emphasizing study. Synagogues were scattered throughout the world, wherever Jews lived. Jerusalem and other large cities had several synagogues. Jews all over the world, though separated from the Temple, continued to be attached to it, and the people longed for the time when they could again worship there.

DISCIPLE FAST TRACK

So the chastisement of Israel at the hands of Assyria and the exile of Judah by the Babylonians now turned the faith of the Jewish people toward a radical obedience. Their experience fortified their belief that the righteous will prosper but the wicked will perish. But even in this era of radical faith and careful obedience, righteousness also embraced the doing of justice.

Day 5—Job

When your class meets, group members will read an excerpt of the Job drama. The excerpt is clear and relatively brief. It contains the major arguments Job's friends used to defend the commonly accepted belief of that time: The righteous prosper; the wicked suffer and perish.

The prologue (Job 1–2) describes an idyllic scene—a righteous man with health, wealth, and children. All of life's blessings seem showered upon a godly man.

They were a happy family—sons taking turns giving dinner parties for one another and for their sisters, Job getting up early the next morning to offer sacrifices of praise to the Lord.

Then, Job's unbelievable wealth—seven thousand sheep, three thousand camels, one thousand oxen, five hundred donkeys—is lost suddenly to enemy raids and natural disaster. Still worse, his sons and daughters all die when a strong wind collapses the house they are in.

Finally Job's own body is afflicted with terrible sores. He sits among the ashes, scraping his sores with a piece of broken pottery. All the promises of piety are shattered: health, wealth, large family, dignity, and honor—all are dramatically taken from God's good man.

The author's use of drama heightens the mystery, the confusion, the conflict in which Job finds himself. Easy answers won't suffice. Job wants something greater than traditional religion. He wants to meet God, face-to-face.

Satan is used dramatically as the cause of all the trouble. (The term *Satan* here is a description of a celestial being who is an adversary of humankind, not of God. This Satan is not the devil of Christian tradition.) The prologue, with its dialogue between Satan and God, is the author's way of establishing the predicament.

Remember that in Job's day people had no concept of life after death. They believed that death took people to a shadowy, vapor-like Sheol. The Job drama points out that justice must be proved in this world. Fairness, if there is fairness, and divine retribution, if there is divine retribution, must occur before death.

The Job Drama

(The following dramatic reading is excerpted from the Good News Translation in Today's English Version [GNT]. It follows the sequence of verses in the Book of Job from Chapter 3 through Chapter 42 but includes only speeches necessary for you to follow the logic of the drama.)

The Old Testament Hebrew word *sa-tan* means opponent, adversary, accuser, attacker. Here in Job it is used with the definite article—*ha-sa-tan,* meaning *the* adversary, *the* accuser. It is not a proper name but the description of a function or role. When the Book of Job was written, probably during the sixth century B.C., the Israelites had no concept of the devil, and their understanding of Satan was quite different from the way Christians today think of Satan. In Job, Satan is not the enemy of God but a kind of official accuser, a member of the heavenly council. His job is to point out specific accusations to God.

During the Exile (587/586–538 B.C.), the Israelites had come into contact with the Persian and Babylonian ideas of two main gods, one good and one evil, competing eternally in the affairs of human beings. They gradually attached this idea to their idea of the figure of Satan, which by about 200 B.C. had developed into a personification of everything opposed to God.

By the time the New Testament was written, people thought of Satan and the devil as the same—the leader of the forces of evil, "the evil one" of Matthew 6:13, tempting human beings to sin, and archenemy of Christ and the church.

JOB: O God, put a curse on the day I was born;
    put a curse on the night when I was conceived!
  Turn that day into darkness, God.
  Never again remember that day;
    never again let light shine on it. . . .
  Keep the morning star from shining;
    give that night no hope of dawn.
  Curse that night for letting me be born,
    for exposing me to trouble and grief.
  I wish I had died in my mother's womb
    or died the moment I was born. . . .
  Instead of eating, I mourn,
    and I can never stop groaning.
  Everything I fear and dread comes true.
  I have no peace, no rest
    and my troubles never end.

ELIPHAZ: Job, will you be annoyed if I speak?
    I can't keep quiet any longer.
  You have taught many people
    and given strength to feeble hands.
  When someone stumbled, weak and tired,
    your words encouraged him to stand.
  Now it's your turn to be in trouble,
    and you are too stunned to face it.
  You worshiped God, and your life was blameless;
    and so you should have confidence and hope.
  Think back now. Name a single case
    where someone righteous met with disaster.
  I have seen people plow fields of evil
    and plant wickedness like seed;
    now they harvest wickedness and evil. . . .
  "Can anyone be righteous in the sight of God
    or be pure before his Creator? . . ."
  Evil does not grow in the soil,
    nor does trouble grow out of the ground.
  No indeed! We bring trouble on ourselves,
    as surely as sparks fly up from a fire.
  If I were you, I would turn to God
    and present my case to him. . . .
  Happy is the person whom God corrects!
  Do not resent it when he rebukes you. . . .

JOB: Why won't God give me what I ask?
    Why won't he answer my prayer?
  If only he would go ahead and kill me!
  If I knew he would, I would leap for joy,
    no matter how great my pain.
  I know that God is holy;
    I have never opposed what he commands. . . .
  All right, teach me; tell me my faults.
    I will be quiet and listen to you.

Honest words are convincing,
　but you are talking nonsense. . . .
But you think I am lying—
　you think I can't tell right from wrong. . . .
When I lie down to sleep, the hours drag;
　I toss all night and long for dawn. . . .

JOB (to God): Remember, O God, my life is only a
　　　breath;
　my happiness has already ended. . . .
No! I can't be quiet!
　I am angry and bitter.
　I have to speak. . . .
Why are people so important to you? . . .
Are you harmed by my sin, you jailer?
　Why use me for your target practice?
　Am I so great a burden to you? . . .
Soon I will be in my grave,
　and I'll be gone when you look for me.

BILDAD: Are you finally through with your windy speech?
　God never twists justice;
　he never fails to do what is right.
Your children must have sinned against God,
　and so he punished them as they deserved.
But turn now and plead with Almighty God;
　if you are so honest and pure,
　then God will come and help you
　and restore your household as your reward.
All the wealth you lost will be nothing
　compared with what God will give you then. . . .

JOB:　Yes, I've heard all that before.
　But how can a human being win a case against God?
How can anyone argue with him?
　He can ask a thousand questions
　that no one could ever answer.
God is so wise and powerful;
　no one can stand up against him. . . .
Though I am innocent, all I can do
　is beg for mercy from God my judge. . . .
If God were human, I could answer him;
　we could go to court to decide our quarrel.
But there is no one to step between us—
　no one to judge both God and me. . . .
Isn't my life almost over? Leave me alone!
　Let me enjoy the time I have left. . . .

ZOPHAR: How I wish God would answer you!
　He would tell you there are many sides to wisdom;
　there are things too deep for human knowledge.
God is punishing you less than you deserve. . . .
God knows which people are worthless;
　he sees all their evil deeds. . . .

Put your heart right, Job. Reach out to God.
Put away evil and wrong from your home.
Then face the world again, firm and courageous. . . .
You will live secure and full of hope;
   God will protect you and give you rest. . . .

JOB: Yes, you are the voice of the people.
     When you die, wisdom will die with you.
  But I have as much sense as you have;
     I am in no way inferior to you;
     everyone knows all that you have said.
  Even my friends laugh at me now;
     they laugh, although I am righteous and blameless;
     but there was a time when God answered my prayers.
  You have no troubles, and yet you make fun of me;
     you hit someone who is about to fall. . . .
  But my dispute is with God, not you;
     I want to argue my case with him. . . .
  I am ready to state my case,
     because I know I am in the right.
  Are you coming to accuse me, God?
     If you do, I am ready to be silent and die.
  Let me ask for two things; agree to them,
     and I will not try to hide from you;
     stop punishing me, and don't crush me with terror.
  Speak first, O God, and I will answer.
     Or let me speak, and you answer me.
  What are my sins? What wrongs have I done?
     What crimes am I charged with? . . .

ELIPHAZ: Empty words, Job! Empty words!
  No one who is wise would talk the way you do
     or defend himself with such meaningless words.
  If you had your way, no one would fear God;
     no one would pray to him.
  Your wickedness is evident by what you say;
     you are trying to hide behind clever words.
  There is no need for me to condemn you;
     you are condemned by every word you speak. . . .
  Why, God does not trust even his angels;
     even they are not pure in his sight.
  And we drink evil as if it were water;
     yes, we are corrupt; we are worthless. . . .

JOB: I have heard words like that before;
     the comfort you give is only torment. . . .
  (to God) You have worn me out, God;
     you have let my family be killed.
     You have seized me; you are my enemy.
  I am skin and bones,
     and people take that as proof of my guilt. . . .

BILDAD: You are only hurting yourself with your anger.
     Will the earth be deserted because you are angry?

Will God move mountains to satisfy you?
The light of the wicked will still be put out;
  its flame will never burn again. . . .

JOB: Even if I have done wrong,
    how does that hurt you?
You think you are better than I am,
    and regard my troubles as proof of my guilt.
Can't you see it is God who has done this? . . .
You are my friends! Take pity on me!
    The hand of God has struck me down.
Why must you persecute me the way God does?
    Haven't you tormented me enough? . . .
But I know there is someone in heaven
    who will come at last to my defense.
Even after my skin is eaten by disease,
    while still in this body I will see God.
I will see him with my own eyes,
    and he will not be a stranger. . . .

ZOPHAR: Surely you know that from ancient times,
    when we humans were first placed on earth,
    no wicked people have been happy for long. . . .

JOB: My quarrel is not with mortals;
    I have good reason to be impatient.
Look at me. Isn't that enough
    to make you stare in shocked silence?
When I think of what has happened to me,
    I am stunned, and I tremble and shake.
Why does God let evil people live,
    let them grow old and prosper?
They have children and grandchildren,
    and live to watch them all grow up.
God does not bring disaster on their homes;
    they never have to live in terror. . . .
And you! You try to comfort me with nonsense!
    Every answer you give is a lie!

ELIPHAZ: Is there any one, even the wisest,
    who could ever be of use to God?
Does your doing right benefit God,
    or does your being good help him at all?
It is not because you stand in awe of God
    that he reprimands you and brings you to trial.
No, it's because you have sinned so much;
    it's because of all the evil you do. . . .

JOB: I still rebel and complain against God;
    I cannot keep from groaning.
How I wish I knew where to find him,
    and knew how to go where he is.
I would state my case before him
    and present all the arguments in my favor.

I want to know what he would say
   and how he would answer me. . . .
I follow faithfully the road he chooses,
   and never wander to either side.
I always do what God commands;
   I follow his will, not my own desires. . . .
   I tremble with fear before him. . . .

BILDAD: Can anyone be righteous or pure in God's sight?
   In his eyes even the moon is not bright,
     or the stars pure.
   Then what about a human being, that worm, that insect?
     What is a human life worth in God's eyes? . . .

JOB: If only my life could once again
     be as it was when God watched over me. . . .
   Almighty God was with me then,
     and I was surrounded by all my children. . . .
   I have always acted justly and fairly.
   I was eyes for the blind,
     and feet for the lame.
   I was like a father to the poor
     and took the side of strangers in trouble.
   I destroyed the power of cruel men
     and rescued their victims. . . .
   Why do you attack a ruined man,
     one who can do nothing but beg for pity?
   Didn't I weep with people in trouble
     and feel sorry for those in need?
   I hoped for happiness and light,
     but trouble and darkness came instead.
   I am torn apart by worry and pain;
     I have had day after day of suffering. . . .
   I swear I have never acted wickedly
     and never tried to deceive others.
   Let God weigh me on honest scales,
     and he will see how innocent I am. . . .

ELIHU: I am young, and you are old,
     so I was afraid to tell you what I think.
   I told myself that you ought to speak,
     that you older men should share your wisdom.
   But it is the spirit of Almighty God
     that comes to us and gives us wisdom.
   It is not growing old that makes men wise
     or helps us to know what is right. . . .
   Now this is what I heard you say:
   "I am not guilty; I have done nothing wrong.
     I am innocent and free from sin.
   But God finds excuses for attacking me
     and treats me like an enemy.
   He binds chains on my feet;
     he watches every move I make."
   But I tell you, Job, you are wrong.

God is greater than any human being.
Why do you accuse God
  of never answering our complaints?
Although God speaks again and again,
  no one pays attention to what he says.
At night when people are asleep,
  God speaks in dreams and visions.
He makes them listen to what he says,
  and they are frightened at his warnings.
God speaks to make them stop their sinning
  and to save them from becoming proud.
He will not let them be destroyed;
  he saves them from death itself.
God corrects us by sending sickness
  and filling our bodies with pain. . . .
God does all this again and again;
  each one saves a person's life,
  and gives him the joy of living. . . .
God's power is so great that we cannot come near him;
  he is righteous and just in his dealings with us.
No wonder, then, that everyone is awed by him,
  and that he ignores those who claim to be wise. . . .

THE LORD *(to Job)*: Who are you to question my wisdom
  with your ignorant, empty words?
Now stand up straight
  and answer the questions I ask you.
Were you there when I made the world?
  If you know so much, tell me about it.
Who decided how large it would be?
  Who stretched the measuring line over it?
  Do you know all the answers?
What holds up the pillars that support the earth?
  Who laid the cornerstone of the world? . . .
Job, you challenged Almighty God;
  will you give up now, or will you answer?

JOB: I spoke foolishly, LORD. What can I answer?
  I will not try to say anything else.
  I have already said more than I should. . . .

THE LORD: Now stand up straight,
  and answer my questions.
Are you trying to prove that I am unjust—
  to put me in the wrong and yourself in the right?
Are you as strong as I am?
  Can your voice thunder as loud as mine?
If so, stand up in your honor and pride;
  clothe yourself with majesty and glory. . . .

JOB: I know, LORD, that you are all-powerful;
  that you can do everything you want.
You ask how I dare question your wisdom
  when I am so very ignorant.

I talked about things I did not understand,
  about marvels too great for me to know.
You told me to listen while you spoke
  and to try to answer your questions.
In the past I knew only what others had told me,
  but now I have seen you with my own eyes.
So I am ashamed of all I have said
  and repent in dust and ashes.

In the end, not counting the epilogue (42:7-17), which was probably designed to put the drama back in the context of traditional Jewish belief, what gave Job his peace of mind?

MARKS OF DISCIPLESHIP

In this lesson we have covered trusting God with our feelings, right living, and handling unexplained suffering.

Mystery often accompanies our suffering. Natural disasters, disease, and the actions of others can cause us great pain. In the face of unexplained suffering, the disciple trusts God. God does not always give us answers; God promises to be with us (Psalm 23).

How are you learning to trust God with all your feelings?

Mark of Discipleship
Disciples trust God with all their thoughts and feelings, strive to live in harmony with God's laws, and trust God in the face of unexplained suffering.

How are you applying the lessons of Proverbs in your life?

How are you able to help others in the midst of unexplained suffering?

IF YOU WANT TO KNOW MORE

The Book of Ecclesiastes battles the same rigid orthodoxy found in Job. The wise old teacher quotes proverbs and then contradicts them from his own observations. If you have time, read Ecclesiastes. Translate *vanity* as meaning "in vain," "futile," or "meaningless." Look especially at Ecclesiastes 7 and 9.

"Look, I am sending my messenger who will clear the path before me; suddenly the LORD whom you are seeking will come to his temple. The messenger of the covenant in whom you take delight is coming, says the LORD of heavenly forces."
—Malachi 3:1

12 People Hope for a Savior

OUR HUMAN CONDITION

We swing between two extremes. Either we drift into cynicism, supposing that evil prospers and death ends all, or we try to convince ourselves that a new government, a change in leadership, or some quick fix will save us. Only special people seem to catch the vision of God's final kingdom of peace. We need and desire something more. So we wait.

ASSIGNMENT

This week's Scriptures will be difficult, for they contain visions, dreams, prophecies, and revelations of end times. The difficulties are compounded by ancient images, deliberately concealed symbols, and scholarly problems. But notice, as we end our study of the Old Testament, that hope is alive and light shines in the darkness.

Pray daily before study:

"God! My God! It's you—
    I search for you!
    My whole being thirsts for you!
    My body desires you
        in a dry and tired land,
        no water anywhere" (Psalm 63:1).

Prayer concerns for the week:

Day 1 Read and complete "The Bible Teaching: Daniel" on pages 102–104.

Day 2 **Read Daniel 1–3** (young Daniel and his three friends, the fiery furnace).

Day 3 **Read Daniel 4–6** (two kings, Daniel in the lions' den).

Day 4 **Read Daniel 7; 10; Isaiah 8:21–9:7; 11:1-10; 42:1-9; Micah 5:2-4** (Messiah and end times, future hope of Israel).

Day 5 **Read Jonah 1–4** (Israel's mission to the world). If you have time, read Esther 1–10. We will not discuss Esther in class, but it is an exciting story. It also reminds us that Jews were scattered all over the world and triumphed over their enemies. If time permits, you can also read Zechariah 9 and Malachi 3–4, which provide clues to the time between the testaments.

Day 6 **Review the timeline of Old Testament biblical history on pages 108–109. Read and complete the questions in "The Bible Teaching: The Time Between the Testaments," pages 104–107.**

Day 7 Rest, pray, and attend class.

Disciple FAST TRACK

THE BIBLE TEACHING: DANIEL

Every Bible student should know these terms:

Apocalypse—prophetic revelation of what is to come, especially end times. Literally, the word means to uncover, to reveal. The Book of Revelation is sometimes called the Apocalypse.

Eschatology—concerned with ultimate or last things, such as death, judgment, heaven, and hell.

Messiah—the anticipated deliverer, the Anointed One who is to come.

Son of Man—Hebrew idiom for "man," symbolizes the coming kingdom as a man in contrast to the past kingdoms symbolized as beasts.

Kingdom of God—different from earthly kingdoms; the concluding time when God will rule in justice, harmony, and peace. The term *kingdom of God* does not appear in the Old Testament, though the concept does.

The Book of Daniel

We have not read some other important parts of the Old Testament. Why read a difficult book like Daniel?

Four reasons:

1. Daniel provides a perspective on Jewish people living in a culture alien to their religious practices and beliefs.

2. Daniel for Jews, like Revelation for Christians, was written to help the faithful "hang on" during persecution.

3. Many Christians see in the Book of Daniel as in other Old Testament passages a glimpse of Messiah, the Anointed One who is to come.

4. A study of Daniel formally introduces us to apocalyptic literature, which takes our thoughts beyond the kingdoms of this world into a concluding kingdom of God and lays groundwork for much New Testament thought. Understanding apocalyptic literature is necessary for understanding the early Christian community.

Certain themes and characteristics typify apocalyptic literature:

Apocalyptic literature reflects the belief that a cosmic struggle is being waged between the forces of good and the forces of evil. This struggle is leading up to a climactic battle in which good will triumph.

Apocalyptic literature emphasizes eschatology, or the study of end times. The "end" usually means the end of a particular age, although it can refer to the end of time as we know it. The basic idea is that the present age is under the influence of evil and that the people of God are suffering persecution. Further, this suffering will increase until God suddenly intervenes on behalf of God's people and inaugurates a new age of peace and joy.

Apocalyptic literature often contains images and symbols that at the time of the writing were meant to be obscure and therefore are difficult for readers in later generations to understand. For example, the image of a horn generally represented power; the color white stood for victory or purity; the term *ancient one* emphasized God's eternity, sovereignty, and wisdom rather than advanced age.

Apocalyptic literature is usually pessimistic about the current world order and regards the intervention of God as the only solution to the problems and suffering of God's people.

Despite its pessimism, apocalyptic literature is designed to give readers a sense of confidence and security. Its primary message is that God is in control and that God's people will ultimately triumph.

Daniel in Babylon

King Nebuchadnezzar of Babylon ravaged Judah, deported the stronger, younger people in 597 B.C. (Ezekiel was one), and finally destroyed Jerusalem and the Temple in 587/586 B.C. Daniel and his young friends were selected to be trained to serve the empire. However, they refused to violate Jewish food laws and refused to worship Babylonian gods, perhaps including images of the kings. Jews in exile have always had to face the difficulty of remaining faithful in an alien culture. The Book of Daniel says, "Be strong!" (10:19). God will be with you. Just as God was with you in the fires of Egypt, so he was with Shadrach, Meshach, and Abednego in the fiery furnace.

Daniel interpreted dreams for Nebuchadnezzar and his successor Belshazzar. Observe that the rulers thought they were all-powerful, but God humbled them. Daniel read the handwriting on the wall: "You've been weighed on the scales, and you don't measure up" (Daniel 5:27).

Be strong; the kingdoms of this world come and go.

The four beasts are thought to refer to kingdoms: the lion (Babylonian Empire), the bear (Median Empire), the leopard (Persian Empire), and the terrifying, dragonlike beast (Greek Empire).

So much of the material in Daniel 7–10 is apocalyptic, visionary, and symbolic that it is difficult to interpret accurately. That is for a reason. Either it was written to prepare the people for times of trouble, or it was written to comfort the people during times of trouble by drawing on past courage and wisdom. Most scholars agree that the Book of Daniel reached its present form during the terrible persecutions of 167–164 B.C. under the Seleucid ruler Antiochus Epiphanes IV.

Under that savage rule, many people were killed. Foreign idols and an altar to Zeus were placed in the Temple, the sacred altar was desecrated, and Jerusalem was sacked. Jews were forbidden to observe Sabbath and dietary laws, to practice circumcision, or to offer sacrifices in the Temple.

Be strong; do not lose heart; remember whose people you are. Will not the God who rescued Daniel from the lions' den save his obedient people even from the jaws of persecution?

Apocalypses

The Messiah, or Anointed One, is foretold in many of the prophets. The one who is to usher in the Kingdom will be "humble and riding on an ass" (Zechariah 9:9). He will be born in Bethlehem and "will stand and shepherd his flock in the strength of the LORD" (Micah 5:2-4). Malachi promised a "messenger who will clear the path before me," who will be "like the refiner's fire" (Malachi 3:1-2). Isaiah of Jerusalem wrote:

> "A child is born to us, a son is given to us,
>   and authority will be on his shoulders.
> He will be named
>   Wonderful Counselor, Mighty God,
>   Eternal Father, Prince of Peace" (Isaiah 9:6).

THE BIBLE TEACHING: THE TIME BETWEEN THE TESTAMENTS

Remember the fall of Jerusalem in 587/86 B.C. to the Babylonians. The Jews were taken into exile and remained there for nearly fifty years. In 539 B.C. the Babylonian Empire crumbled under the Persians led by Cyrus II. This is the beginning of the Persian period.

The Persian Period (539–333 B.C.)

In 538 B.C. Cyrus II issued an edict allowing the exiled Jews to return to Jerusalem to rebuild the Temple. Some Jews acted immediately to get back to Jerusalem; others followed later, some as much as one hundred years later.

The initial return from Babylon after the edict of Cyrus was led by Sheshbazzar, who began the rebuilding of the Temple but did not complete it.

The second return was led by Zerubbabel and Jeshua during the reign of Darius I (521–485 B.C.). They built an altar and reestablished the sacrificial system in Jerusalem. Under the influence of Haggai and Zechariah, Zerubbabel and Jeshua finished the Temple (515 B.C.).

Ezra came to Jerusalem much later during the reign of Artaxerxes I (464–423 B.C.). He brought with him from the Babylonian Jewish community their form of the Mosaic law and instituted it. According to the Book of Nehemiah, Nehemiah returned twice during this same period to rebuild the walls of Jerusalem and to insist on religious reform.

Still later, during the reign of Artaxerxes II (404–358 B.C.), a fourth group returned, led by Nehemiah.

Ezra the priest and Nehemiah the layman were tough. They had to be. They faced opposition from the mixed peoples living in and around Jerusalem and walked a political tightrope with Persia.

As Nehemiah said of his laborers, they rebuilt the walls of Jerusalem with a weapon in one hand and building materials in the other (Nehemiah 4:17-18).

Although many Jews returned, the majority did not. This fact is especially important. Several million Jews were scattered all over the Mediterranean world. By the third century B.C., an estimated one million Jews lived in Egypt alone. Think for a minute. At the time of the beginning of the return from Babylonian exile (538 B.C.), some Jews had been exiled from the Northern Kingdom for nearly two hundred years; others, from the Southern Kingdom for two or three generations. They now had jobs, businesses, or they were slaves. They had families, often no money, and had become a part of other cultures and climates. Besides, the economic conditions back home were bleak indeed. Why go back?

Jonah

The message of Jonah insists that Israel is to be a light to the Gentiles. A nondescript prophet named Jonah was under orders to go to Nineveh (the capital of the old Assyrian Empire, symbolizing the heart of "the enemy") and warn the Ninevites of impending doom. Like Israel, Jonah resisted. The miracle in the story is that Nineveh repented. The writer of Jonah, through story, stands in tension with the rigid orthodoxy of Ezra. How would you describe, in your own words, that tension between "separateness" (Ezra) and "missionary zeal" (Jonah)?

The Greek Period (333–198 B.C.)

An important date, and easy to remember, is 333 B.C. Alexander the Great won a decisive victory at Issus over the Persians and began to establish Greek influence throughout the known world. Alexander's goals were cultural. His armies spread Greek language, Greek culture, and Greek religion everywhere.

The common language in Palestine under the Babylonians and Persians had become Aramaic. But now every educated person was influenced to speak and write Greek. People moved about more freely. Trade flourished.

Sporting events, in which athletes participated without clothing, became popular everywhere. The nakedness was abhorrent to the Jews. Circumcision became an issue. Some Jewish men had surgery to remove signs of circumcision so they could compete in athletic events without ridicule.

The existence of many Greek gods and philosophies fostered an atmosphere of tolerance and freedom for Jewish religion. Dialogue and debate over philosophical, ethical, and religious matters were common. Many Greeks were drawn to the concept of one supreme Creator God. Some non-Jews under Greek influence studied Judaism and became "God-fearers" or Gentile believers. Some became converts to Judaism.

The Period of the Seleucids (198–167 B.C.)

After the death of Alexander the Great, the Greek Empire split into four parts. Antiochus IV came to rule (175–163 B.C.), calling himself Epiphanes, "god manifest." This cruel king cracked down hard on the Jews. He forced cultural and religious conformity. He demanded worship of himself as Zeus and built an altar to Zeus in the Jerusalem Temple. He even slaughtered a pig (unclean in Jewish ritual) on the altar.

DISCIPLE FAST TRACK

He also
- confiscated valuables from the Temple in Jerusalem;
- appointed the highest bidder to the office of high priest;
- rewarded Jews who cooperated with his government;
- called in his troops to put down resistance;
- burned copies of Jewish law;
- outlawed circumcision under penalty of death;
- outlawed sabbath observances and food laws, forcing Jews to eat pork.

In Daniel 7—12, he is the little horn of 7:8, 20-27; 8:9-14; and in 11:31 he is "the abomination that makes desolate."

The Hasmonean Period (167–63 B.C.)

Under the leadership of the Maccabean family, some Jews took up arms against Antiochus and after violent warfare established a century of Jewish independence.

Roman Rule (63 B.C. and Beyond)

Roman control over Palestine began in 63 B.C. and flourished under Caesar Augustus, who was emperor from 31 B.C. to A.D. 14. As we read the New Testament, we tend to emphasize Roman brutality because of Herod the Great, who became a "puppet king" loyal to Rome. But the world experienced the *Pax Romana* (the peace of Rome) for nearly two hundred years. Roman engineers built roads to the farthest reaches of the empire. Later, Christian missionaries like Barnabas and Paul traveled easily because of that peace and those roads, spreading the gospel in a few short years throughout the Mediterranean world.

Taxation under Greeks and Romans was severe, arbitrary, and corrupt. Wealthy people (like Zacchaeus in Luke 19:1-10) bid for the right to be "tax farmers." For a price, Rome gave them territories. They hired other people to work as collectors. These "publicans" collected head taxes and property taxes on slaves, cattle, buildings, and so on. They set their rate with few guidelines, paid Rome the required fee, and kept everything else they collected. Jewish tax collectors were considered "sinners" and unclean, not only because of their greed but because of their contact with Gentiles.

Religious Life

Jews in exile (the Diaspora) had no Temple, no formal priesthood; they simply met together. So another form of religious life emerged: *synagogue. Synagogue* meant "a gathering," but it came to mean "a place of prayer." Jews, dispersed all over the world, met in synagogues in town after town, city after city.

What happened at synagogue? People met regularly for prayer and study. Lay teachers called rabbis emerged. Children were taught their language, their customs, their laws, and their rituals. Sabbath worship, consisting of prayer and reading of Scripture with teaching and discussion, was conducted.

The synagogue provided welfare for indigent Jews. It was a political and social center for life in the Jewish community.

NOTES

As the centuries just before the New Testament time unfolded, the law of Moses became increasingly important. The Law sometimes meant Torah (the first five books of the Old Testament), but often it referred to the entire law with all of the oral traditions and interpretations.

The Law was elevated, praised, glorified. Ezra established the law of Moses squarely at the heart of Judaism. So did the rabbis. The goal was to obey the Law in every detail and to live perfectly before God. Long before the Temple was destroyed by the Romans in A.D. 70, sacrifice at the Temple was less important than study of the Law in the synagogue.

Several religious groups developed within Judaism during the time between the testaments: scribes, Sadducees, Pharisees, Essenes, and Zealots.

MARKS OF DISCIPLESHIP

Disciples sense their unity with the historic people of God (descendants of Abraham and Sarah) and bring that understanding to their hearing of the gospel of Jesus Christ. Disciples keep the dream alive and live in hope with a vision of God's kingdom.

In what ways are you beginning to understand the unity of the Bible and the central theme of salvation history?

Mark of Discipleship
Disciples hear the gospel of Jesus Christ in the context of unity with the historic people of God.

IF YOU WANT TO KNOW MORE

If you have time, read Haggai, Zechariah, and Malachi. These writings provide glimpses into the time between the testaments, and Malachi is an eloquent and revealing link between the older prophetic era and the emerging form of Judaism.

First Maccabees in the Apocrypha would be appropriate reading to get some history of the time between the testaments.

Memorize titles of the New Testament books.

TIMELINE OF OLD TESTAMENT BIBLICAL HISTORY

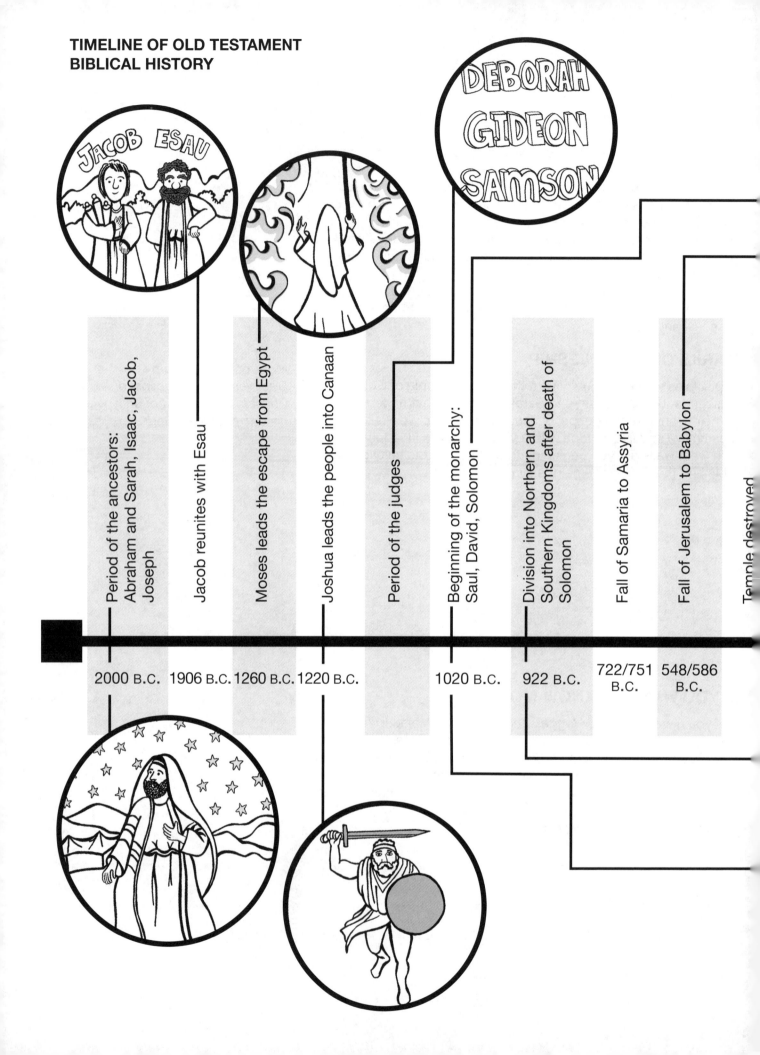

Period of the ancestors: Abraham and Sarah, Isaac, Jacob, Joseph

Jacob reunites with Esau

Moses leads the escape from Egypt

Joshua leads the people into Canaan

Period of the judges

Beginning of the monarchy: Saul, David, Solomon

Division into Northern and Southern Kingdoms after death of Solomon

Fall of Samaria to Assyria

Fall of Jerusalem to Babylon

Temple destroyed

2000 B.C.   1906 B.C. 1260 B.C. 1220 B.C.   1020 B.C.   922 B.C.   722/751 B.C.   548/586 B.C.

Persian Period

Edict of Cyrus

Return of exiles

Temple rebuilt

Greek Period

Alexander the Great

Jews revolt (Hasmonean Period)

Romans capture Jerusalem

Herod the Great appointed king over Palestine

Birth of Jesus

539 B.C.   538 B.C.   515 B.C.   333 B.C.   167 B.C.   63 B.C.   37 B.C.   4 B.C.

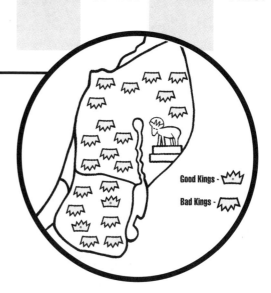

To download and print this timeline, go to *adultbiblestudies.com/fasttrack*.